RECEIVED

APR 7 2003

BY:_____

No Longer the Property of
Hayner Public Library District

HAYNER PLD/ALTON SQUARE

HAYNER PUBLIC LIBRARY DISTRICT
ALTON, ILLINOIS

OVERDUES 10 PER DAY MAXIMUM FINE
COST OF BOOKS. LOST OR DAMAGED
BOOKS ADDITIONAL $5.00 SERVICE CHARGE

THE PARTHENON

MARY BEARD

HARVARD UNIVERSITY PRESS

Cambridge, Massachusetts

2003

HAYNER PUBLIC LIBRARY DISTRICT

ALTON, ILLINOIS

Copyright © 2002 by Mary Beard
All rights reserved

First published in Great Britain in 2002 by
Profile Books Ltd

CIP data is available from the Library of Congress

ISBN 0-674-01085-X

Endpaper engraving taken from J. Stuart and N. Revett,
Antiquities of Athens II, London, 1787 (1789).

938.5
BEA

AEI-9265

CONTENTS

The most beautiful things in the world are there [Athens] ... The sumptuous temple of Athena stands out and is well worth a look. It is called the Parthenon and is on the hill above the theatre. It makes a tremendous impression on visitors.

                              Heracleides of Crete (third century BC)

Reporter: 'Did you visit the Parthenon during your trip to Greece?'

Shaquille O'Neal (US basketball star): 'I can't really remember the names of the clubs we went to.'

1. Not everyone goes misty-eyed when confronted with the Parthenon. Here the Hungarian dancer Nikolska poses among its columns in 1929. Isadora Duncan had tried the same trick a few years earlier.

....

WHY THE PARTHENON MIGHT
MAKE YOU CRY

THE REAL THING

When Sigmund Freud first visited the Parthenon in 1904, he was surprised to discover that it really did exist, 'just as we learnt at school'. It had taken Freud some time to summon the nerve to make a visit, and he wrote vividly of the uncomfortable hours of indecision that he spent in Trieste, trying to resolve whether to catch the steamer to Athens or sail to Corfu as he had originally planned. When he finally arrived and climbed up to the ruins on the Acropolis, delight was mixed with shock. It was as if – or so he later tailored the story – he had been walking beside Loch Ness, had spotted the legendary Monster stranded on the shore and so been driven to admit that it wasn't just a myth after all. 'It really *does* exist.' Not all admirers of the Parthenon have had the courage to follow Freud. One of those not prepared to take the risk of seeing for himself was Werner Jaeger, a renowned classical scholar of the early twentieth century and passionate advocate of the humanising power of ancient Greek culture. Jaeger got as far as Athens at least once, but he drew the line at climbing up to the ruined temple itself – dreading that the 'real thing' might not live up to his expectations.

2. A quiet day on the Acropolis. Hundreds of thousands of visitors flock to
the site each year. Currently the Parthenon itself is off-limits while more
than twenty years of restoration work – signalled here by the crane inside the
building – is carried out (pp. 114–15).

Jaeger need not have worried. There have been few tourists over the last 200 years or more who have not managed to be impressed by the Parthenon and its dramatic setting on the Athenian Acropolis: intrepid travellers in the late eighteenth century braved wars, bandits and some very nasty bugs to catch their first glimpse of 'real' Greek architecture and sculpture; a whole array of politicians and cultural superstars from Bernard Shaw to Bill Clinton have competed to be photographed, misty-eyed, between the Parthenon's columns (*Illustration 1*); busloads of everyday visitors, in still increasing numbers, make this the centrepiece of their Athenian pilgrimage, eagerly hanging on to the archaeological minutiae regurgitated by their guides. It is true, of course, that tourists are cannily adept at convincing themselves that they are having a good time, and the cultural pressure on us to be impressed, in retrospect at least, by what-we-think-we-should-be-impressed-by may be almost irresistible. All the same, it is often the case that even the most celebrated wonders of world culture are tinged with disappointment when you meet them face to face: the Mona Lisa is irritatingly small; the Pyramids would be much more atmospheric if they were not on the fringes of the Cairo suburbs, and rather too mundanely serviced by an on-site branch of Pizza Hut. Not so the Parthenon. Against all the odds – the inescapable sun, the crowds of people, the surly guards blowing their whistles at any deviants who try to stray from the prescribed route around the site and, for more than a decade now, the barrage of scaffolding – the Parthenon seems to work for almost everyone, almost every time (*Illustration 2*).

At first sight, then, the modern story of this monument is one told in glowing superlatives. An enterprising businessman-cum-papal diplomat from Ancona set the tone in the fifteenth century, when he visited Athens in 1436: among the huge collections of 'incredible marble buildings … what pleased me most of all,' he wrote, 'was the great and marvellous temple of Pallas Athena on the topmost citadel of the city, a divine work by Phidias, which has 58 towering columns, each seven feet in diameter, and is splendidly adorned with the noblest images on all sides'. Later writers and critics have piled on the eulogies. Predictably perhaps, the antiquarian visitors of the late eighteenth and early nineteenth centuries drooled over the Parthenon's 'exquisite symmetry', its 'glorious fabric' and the 'harmonious analogy of its proportions'. Why beat about the bush? 'It is the most unrivalled triumph of sculpture and architecture that the world ever saw,' was the confident conclusion of Edward Dodwell in 1819, recently returned from three trips to Greece. But a hundred years later Le Corbusier, the most famous prophet of twentieth-century modernism, was still working from very much the same script when he rooted his new vision of architecture in the sheer perfection of the Parthenon. 'There has been nothing like it anywhere or at any period', he wrote in his manifesto, *Towards a New Architecture* (which is illustrated with no fewer than 20 photographs or drawings of the building, some memorably juxtaposed with its modern analogue as a triumph of design, the motor car). And on another occasion he reflected, in more characteristically modernist tones, that 'one clear image will stand in my mind for ever: the Parthenon, stark, stripped, economical, violent, a clamorous outcry against a landscape of grace and terror'.

Almost inevitably, this enthusiasm has been followed by emulation. Right across the western world you can find clones of the Parthenon in all sizes and materials, adapted to a disconcerting range of different functions: from miniature silver cufflinks, through postmodern toasters (the ultimate in kitchenware 1996, courtesy of sculptor Darren Lago), to full-scale, walk-in concrete replicas. The most ostentatious of all is the Walhalla near Regensburg in Germany, brainchild of Ludwig I of Bavaria and intended as a 'Monument of German Unity'. The majority of the designs submitted to Ludwig were based on the Parthenon in one way or another. But the commission eventually went to a vast scheme by the architect Leo von Klenze, set on the top of a wooded 'Acropolis', Bavarian style: the outside an overblown Parthenon, the inside a Teutonic extravaganza, complete with Valkyries and busts of German worthies, from Alaric to Goethe (and now up to, and beyond, Konrad Adenauer). Not all projects came to such lavish fruition. In 1816 the city of Edinburgh, optimistically nicknamed the Athens of the North, was encouraged by none other than Lord Elgin to commemorate the Battle of Waterloo with a lookalike Parthenon on Calton Hill – but got no further than a dozen columns before the money ran out in 1829. These have stood as Edinburgh's pride, or disgrace, ever since, and high-tech plans to finish the job in glass and laser as a gesture to the new millennium were resoundingly rejected by the local residents.

Meanwhile, as the craze for classical style swamped the USA in the nineteenth and early twentieth centuries, the Parthenon was resurrected in the shape of a whole series of

3. The full-size replica of the statue of Athena from the Nashville Parthenon, by Alan LeQuire (seen here by the goddess's right leg). This version of Pheidias' creation was unveiled in 1990 and has won many plaudits for its archaeological accuracy. But visitors must use their imaginations to recreate the appearance of gold and ivory. LeQuire had to settle for the more economical gypsum cement and fibreglass.

government buildings, banks and museums. Pride of place here, for accuracy of reconstruction at least (reputedly correct to three millimetres), goes to the Parthenon in Nashville, Tennessee – the Athens of the South, as it sometimes likes to be known. This started life as a wood, plaster and brick pavilion, built for the Tennessee Centennial Exposition in 1897. But the people of Nashville were so taken with it that it remained in place long after the end of the fair and was rebuilt in more durable concrete in the 1920s; its massive 13-metre statue of the goddess Athena, a replica of what we think once stood in the original building in Athens, was eventually unveiled in 1990 (*Illustration 3*). This Parthenon reached a wider international audience through Robert Altman's movie *Nashville*, his epic satire on the tawdriness of the American dream, showbiz and politics. The final scenes of the film are set among its columns draped with the American flag, where a country-and-western benefit concert is being staged for a no-hope fringe candidate in a presidential election; a characteristically American occasion culminating in a characteristically American murder, as the lead singer is gunned down on the Parthenon's portico by an apparently motiveless assassin. Athenian classicism meets the Stars and Stripes.

'THE BLOODY PARTHENON, I SUPPOSE ...'

There have been, it is true, a few maverick voices raised over the centuries against the general chorus of admiration for the Parthenon. A number of visitors have felt able to confess that the first sight of the building was not quite what they had expected. Winston Churchill, for example, would have liked to see a few more of the collapsed columns re-erected, and was tempted (for he was First Sea Lord at the time) to volunteer a squadron of the British Navy for the task; while Oscar Wilde's charismatic teacher from Trinity College Dublin, J. P. Mahaffy, theorised that any monument so famous was bound to be a bit disappointing when you first saw it ('no building on earth can sustain the burden of such greatness') – before going on to reassure his readers that, if they persevered to a second glance, the 'glory' of the Parthenon and the brilliance of the 'master minds which produced this splendour' would quickly become apparent. Just occasionally you can find some more consistently barbed attempts to take the monument down a peg or two. American novelist Walker Percy must have enjoyed the frisson of transgression when he picked on the Parthenon as a model of modern boredom ('It is a bore. Few people even bother to look – it looked better in the brochure') and fantasised about its total destruction under a massive Soviet attack. At least, he wrote, if you were a NATO colonel 'in a bunker in downtown Athens, binoculars propped on sandbags', watching out for a direct hit on the portico, you wouldn't find the Parthenon *boring*. William Golding was presumably thinking along similar lines when, one March afternoon in the 1960s, after a good Athenian lunch with a classicist friend, he opted to visit 'the bloody Parthenon, I suppose'. It was half-raining, with terrific gusts of wind; the dust blew in their faces, making the usual style of wide-eyed tourism difficult and painful. Golding stopped at the building, looked at it briefly, blew his nose aggressively then – finding a comfortable block of marble – sat down, back to the monument, and stared away from it at the 'industrial gloom of the Piraeus' and the cement works of Eleusis that are just visible from the Athenian Acropolis. 'Beaming euphorically … he said at last, "Now *this* is what I call the right way to look at the Parthenon."'

By and large, however, even the most acerbic cultural critics, the nineteenth- and twentieth-centuries' sharpest tongues, have treated the Parthenon as somehow 'off-limits'. Oscar Wilde, from whom we might reasonably have expected a well-honed quip at the monument's expense, seems hardly even to have shared his professor's doubts about those awkward first impressions. Mahaffy had taken Wilde to Greece in 1877, in the hope that the treasures of pagan antiquity would dissuade his pupil from converting to Catholicism. This campaign against 'Popery' was, if anything, rather too successful – to judge from Wilde's reaction to the Parthenon (as reported, curiously, in a best-selling novel penned by one of his lady friends): 'He spoke to her of the Parthenon, the one temple – not a building – a temple, as complete, as personal as a statue. And that first sight of the Acropolis, the delicate naked columns rising up in the morning sunshine; "It was like coming upon some white Greek goddess …"' A few years later he turned his admiration for the building into such scandalously steamy verses that at least one late-Victorian reader excised them – literally, with her scissors – from the collection in which they appeared. Entitled 'Charmides', the offending poem features 'a Grecian lad' who manages to get himself locked into a temple at dusk, to undress the statue of the goddess Athena and kiss her till dawn: 'Never I ween did lover hold such tryst,/ For all night long he murmured honeyed word,/ And saw her sweet unravished limbs, and kissed/ Her pale and argent body undisturbed'. The temple in which all this takes place, needless to say, bears a striking resemblance to the Parthenon.

Perhaps even more surprising is Virginia Woolf's undiluted enthusiasm for the Parthenon, which she visited in 1906 and again in 1932. Woolf can almost always be relied upon for a caustic comment or two. True to form, in her Greek diaries she is characteristically sharp about the other tourists: the 'hordes of Teutons' and the French, who are notoriously reluctant to take a bath. And she has no more time than most visitors of her generation for the inhabitants of modern Greece. This was long before postcards of smiling, toothless peasants had become a major weapon in the armoury of the Greek tourist industry, selling in vast numbers to sentimental northern Europeans in search of the rustic simplicity of traditional Mediterranean life. For Woolf and her fellows, the peasants were generally dull and stupid, Greeks of all classes 'dirty, ignorant & unstable as water'. But the Parthenon itself, to which she paid daily homage throughout her time in Athens, was an entirely different matter. For once, she claims to have been lost for words: 'our minds had been struck inarticulate by something too great for them to grasp'. And she struggles desperately – and rather ostentatiously, it must be said – to capture on paper the impact of the great monument: its colour is, by turns, bright 'red', 'creamy white', 'rosy', 'tawny', 'ashy pale' (Evelyn Waugh faced the same problem, but likened it more imaginatively to a mild Stilton cheese); 'its columns spring up like fair round limbs, flushed with health'; it 'overcomes you; it is so large, & so strong, & so triumphant'; 'no place seems more lusty & alive than this platform of ancient dead stone'. Or, put more crisply in the novel *Jacob's Room*, where she reworked some of her Athenian experiences, it 'appears likely to outlast the entire world'. Face to face with the Parthenon even Mrs Woolf seems to have gone weak at the knees.

THE CRYING GAME

At least she did not cry – unlike many of the world's most famous critics and connoisseurs, who have found that the Parthenon can reduce them to tears, stiff upper-lip or not. 'The Parthenon is so shattering that it made me weep, which I don't usually do under these circumstances', wrote Cyril Connolly, archly, after a visit in the 1920s. Thousands of others have made a similar confession (or boast), before and since. It is, in fact, a fair guess that more people have wept on the Athenian Acropolis than at any other monument anywhere in the world, with the possible exception of the Taj Mahal. But it is not only aesthetic overload, the shock of anticipation fulfilled or (as a cynic might suspect) showmanship that bring tears to the eyes. Rabindranath Tagore, the Indian poet, composer of the Indian national anthem and compulsive world traveller, is said to have cried at the sheer 'barbarian ugliness' of the ruins he saw on the Acropolis – a useful reminder, if such were needed, that the Parthenon might not look so rosy from a multi-cultural perspective. And there is, of course, a whole tradition, flamboyantly launched by Lord Byron, that makes tears obligatory on the Acropolis, not for the overwhelming beauty of the Parthenon, but for its tragic ruin and for what he saw as its horrible dismemberment.

For the Parthenon is no longer to be found only in Athens. Replicas aside, a good proportion of the sculpture that decorated the original fifth-century BC monument (not to mention a few column capitals and other stray architectural fragments) is now scattered through the museums of Europe. Roughly half the sculpture is housed in Athens, not – as in Byron's day – on the Parthenon itself, but safely away from the notorious Athenian pollution in nearby museums and storerooms. Most of the rest is in the British Museum, London, courtesy of Thomas Bruce, 7th Earl of Elgin, who sold it to the British government in 1816 – including over 75 metres of the famous sculpted 'frieze' that once ran round the whole building, as well as 15 of the 92 sculpted panels (or 'metopes') that were originally displayed high up above the columns and 17 life-size figures that once stood in the temple gables (or 'pediments') (*Figures 1 and 2*). But there is also a notable clutch of material in Paris, including a metope and a slab of frieze, acquired in Athens by a fanatical aristocratic collector in the 1780s, sequestered by the French revolutionaries and now on display in the Louvre, plus various odd, smaller pieces in Copenhagen, Wurzburg, Palermo, Rome, Heidelberg, Vienna, Munich and Strasbourg, mostly pocketed (literally) by early visitors to the Acropolis.

Byron's particular target was Lord Elgin, British ambassador to Constantinople between 1799 and 1803, who had his boatloads of Parthenon sculpture removed from the site through the first decade of the nineteenth century. Some of this had already fallen from its original position and was picked up from the ground near by. But a considerable quantity was removed from the building itself, which involved a whole series of awkward operations, prising the sculpture out or occasionally dismantling small sections of the building to release it. Much of it then turned out to be colossally heavy

FRIEZE   METOPES   PEDIMENT

Figure 1. Position of the sculpture on the Parthenon.

and almost impossible to transport safely, so to lighten the load (and without, so far as we can tell, attacking the sculpted surfaces themselves) Elgin's agents proceeded to saw off the backs of the thickest slabs, removing as much excess weight as they could. All of this was immediately controversial. What Elgin's motives were, and whether he had the legal authority to do what he did, remain, as we shall see in later chapters, matters of intense and irresolvable dispute. The conclusions you reach – whether now or 200 years ago – depend less on facts or logic than on the prejudices from which you start. Predictably, over the centuries, Elgin has been characterised with equal fervour as a parody 'milord' prepared to desecrate the acme of world architecture in search of some nice sculpture to prettify his ancestral seat, and as a selfless hero who practically bankrupted himself in preserving for posterity masterpieces that would otherwise have been ground up for cement by ignorant locals, caught in the crossfire of some internecine war or, in due course, destroyed by acid rain. Neither version has much to recommend it.

Byron never met Elgin and was not present while the sculptures were being removed from the Parthenon. In fact, he would have been hardly more than 13 years old when Elgin's men started their work. He did not set foot in Athens until Christmas Day 1809, when he stayed for 10 weeks, lodging with the famous Widow Macri, whose renowned hospitality extended to taking in a few well-heeled paying guests. He apparently divided his time between deploring the state of modern Athens, touring the sights (you can still just see where he scratched his name on one of the columns of the little temple of Poseidon at Sounion, outside Athens) and scribbling poetry. This included vitriolic attacks on Elgin as well as the ghastly doggerel entitled 'Maid of Athens' in honour of Macri's 12-year-old daughter – 'Maid of Athens, ere we part,/ Give, oh, give me back my heart!/ Or, since that has left my breast,/ Keep it now, and take the rest!'

It is far from clear what exactly lay behind the sheer nastiness of his campaign against Elgin and the export of the sculpture (no insults were spared, not even sideswipes at Elgin's retarded son or carefully placed hints about syphilis and Lady Elgin's adultery). Byron had not yet decided to parade himself as the champion of Greece and Greek freedom – a cause for which he would eventually die, from fever rather than cannon fire, at Missolonghi. Besides, he had all manner of intimate connections with Elgin's men in Athens. On his return visit to Greece, just a few weeks after the first, he had a whirlwind affair with the young brother-in-law of the man who had actually supervised the removal of Elgin's marbles from the Parthenon. And when he finally left for home he was happy enough to travel as far as Malta on the very same boat as the last consignment of marbles, which were also on their way to England after years of delay. But whatever drove Byron's hostility, there can be no doubt that his verses were hugely influential on the reactions to the Parthenon, especially the reactions of the British. 'Cold is the heart, fair Greece! that looks on thee,/ Nor feels as lovers o'er the dust they lov'd;/ Dull is the eye that will not weep to see/ Thy walls defac'd, thy mouldering shrines remov'd/ By British hands …' *Dull is the eye that will not weep*. It was hardly less than an order to greet the Parthenon with tears.

The diaspora of the marbles, and in particular the Elgin collection now in the British Museum, gives another significant spin to the modern story of the Parthenon. From the very moment that the first shipment went on display to the favoured few in 1807 (in a shed behind Elgin's house at the corner of Park Lane in London), the Elgin Marbles have attracted as much attention as the Parthenon itself, if not more. Some reactions to this sculpture chime in closely with the kind of enthusiasm for the building that we have already traced. Mrs Siddons, the celebrity actress of the moment, predictably (and histrionically) shed a tear when she first caught sight of the figures from the temple gables in the Park Lane shed. John Keats swooned on paper, in the shape of a sonnet titled 'On Seeing the Elgin Marbles', when he visited the sculptures in 1817, just after they had been moved to the British Museum, and he is supposed to have incorporated various vignettes taken directly from the frieze in his even more famous 'Ode on a Grecian Urn'. (*Illustration 4*). Goethe meanwhile celebrated the British government's decision to buy the collection from Elgin as 'the beginning of a new age for Great Art'. One of the most quoted reactions of all came from the sculptor, Antonio Canova who turned down Elgin's offer of the plum job of restoring the marbles on the grounds that 'it would be a sacrilege in him or any man to presume to touch them with a chisel'. It is not often pointed out, though, that he contrived this elegant and flattering refusal to his no doubt pressing client some years before he had actually seen the collection with his own eyes.

These sculptures were replicated all over Europe and beyond. You can find a copy of the Parthenon frieze adding

4. This particular scene from the Parthenon frieze is often thought to lie behind John Keats's famous lines in his 'Ode on a Grecian Urn': 'Who are these coming to the sacrifice? To what green altar, O mysterious priest,/ Leadest thou that heifer lowing at the skies ... ?'

classical lustre to the monumental screen at London's Hyde Park Corner, designed by Decimus Burton in the 1820s – who went on, appropriately enough, to emblazon the façade of his building for the brand new Athenaeum Club with another version of this masterpiece from ancient Athens. Exact replicas in the form of plaster casts also flooded out from the British Museum to other museums, schools, art colleges and foreign governments. The Treasury obviously decided that the marbles were a useful tool in diplomatic relations and promptly sent a free gift of a full replica set to the royal courts of Tuscany, Rome, Naples and Prussia (with a smaller selection being packed off, also as a present, to Venice). The Prince Regent gave copies of the whole collection to both Plymouth and Liverpool. Others had to pay for the privilege: in St Petersburg, Bavaria and Wurtemburg royalty dug deep into their pockets for 'parts of the Elgin Marbles'; the Dresden Museum, more economically, swapped a surplus-to-requirements original classical statue for a set of Parthenon casts. It is reckoned that by the mid-nineteenth century there was hardly a sizeable town in Europe or North America that did not somewhere possess the cast of at least one of Elgin's marbles. Private customers, of course, might prefer something on a smaller scale. Almost as soon as the collection arrived in England, the sculptor John Henning cornered, and flooded, the market with miniature boxed sets of plaster replicas of the frieze – still on sale through the British Museum shop even today ('superb as a paperweight or as a miniature focal point for a wall', as the catalogue helpfully suggests).

But, for all this admiration, there is – and always has been – a much stronger dissident tradition on the Elgin Marbles than on the ruins of the Parthenon itself. To start with, it was to do with 'the shock of the new'. Fashionable art theorists in the early 1800s held that art had reached a state of absolute perfection in classical Greece of the fifth century BC. Or so, at least, they judged from what Greek and Roman writers had to say and from later, Roman copies of earlier master-pieces. For, so long as travel to Greece itself remained an exotic and dangerous activity, almost none of those in north-ern Europe who pontificated about the history of art had actually seen an original work of fifth-century Greek sculp-ture. The Elgin Marbles were the first examples of sculpture from what was believed to be the Golden Age of Art that most people in Britain had ever clapped eyes on. If some critics enthused, others did not much like what they saw. Many of the pieces, they thought, were disappointingly bat-tered; a few (especially among the metope panels) seemed frankly second rate and hardly any reached that level of 'sub-limity' they had expected. One notoriously damning judge-ment, trumpeted by a rival collector, Richard Payne Knight, was that Elgin's marbles were not fifth-century BC Greek at all, but Roman additions to the Parthenon from the second century AD. Like Canova, though, Payne Knight spoke before he had seen; he first uttered this put-down, at dinner with Lord Elgin, before the sculptures had even been removed from their crates.

Even after the Roman theory had been decisively scotched, there continued to be voices raised against the star billing of the Elgin Marbles. The sculpture came to stand for all that was worst, as well as best, about classical art: just a little too perfect, slightly sterile, spoiled by the very homo-geneity of the figures and the lack of real-life expression on the faces. Thomas Carlyle, for example, was thinking of the characters depicted on the great frieze when he teased the painter G. F. Watts (who kept some casts of the marbles in his studio): 'There's not a clever man amongst them all, and I would away with them – into space.' And just this kind of dissatisfaction is captured, decades later, in the opening to one of the most influential books on the ancient world to be published in the twentieth century, E. R. Dodds's *The Greeks and the Irrational* (a brilliant exploration of the murkier, 'primitive' aspects of Greek culture). Dodds begins his first chapter with the story of a chance encounter in front of the Parthenon sculptures in the British Museum: '… a young man came up to me and said with a worried air, "I know it's an awful thing to confess, but this Greek stuff doesn't move me one bit … it's all so terribly rational."' It was in response to this complaint, so his story goes, that *The Greeks and the Irrational* was conceived.

DID BYRON GET IT RIGHT?

Other visitors have felt that the sculptures were simply 'wrong' in the British Museum. This was partly a sense that works of art created for the bright Athenian sunshine were inevitably deadened by their display in the sombre atmosphere of Bloomsbury – the English weather outside, the hushed tones adopted by troops of dutiful visitors inside. Virginia Woolf, for one, preferred the 'hairy, tawny bodies' of Greek tragedy to those delicately 'posed on granite plinths in the pale corridors of the British Museum', while 'being brought to the gloom/ Of this dark room' was the main gripe of the marbles themselves, as ventriloquised by Thomas

Hardy in his poem 'Christmas in the Elgin Room'. But these questions of display have, more often than not, been subsumed into what has become the longest-running cultural controversy in the world: should Elgin ever have removed the marbles from their original location? Should they ever have been shipped to Britain? Does justice demand that they be sent back 'home'? In short, did Byron get it right?

These debates have now been running for 200 years. Insults have been traded and a lot more tears have been shed – notably by the formidable Greek Minister of Culture Melina Mercouri, who wept memorably to camera when she visited the marbles in the British Museum in 1983. There have been bad arguments on both sides. Britain has been parodied as an unreconstructed colonial power, desperate to hang on to its cultural booty in place of its lost empire; Greece as a jumped-up Balkan republic, a peasant state hardly to be trusted with the stewardship of an international treasure. Politicians have leapt on and off the bandwagon. Successive Greek governments have found the loss of the Parthenon sculptures a convenient symbol of national unity, and demands for their restitution a low-cost and relatively risk-free campaign. With equal expediency, successive Labour governments in Britain have forgotten the rash promises they made in opposition to return the marbles to Athens just as soon as they reached power. Meanwhile, in the cross-fire, all kinds of crucial questions of cultural heritage have been raised: to whom does the Parthenon, and other such world-class monuments, belong? Should cultural treasures be repatriated, or should museums be proud of their international holdings? Is the Parthenon a special case – and why?

Whatever the rights and wrongs of this dispute (and they are much trickier to judge than campaigners would have us believe), the unquenchable controversy has had one very clear effect. It has helped to keep the Parthenon at the very top of our cultural agenda. Not single-handedly, of course. The Parthenon belongs, as we have already seen, to that elite band of monuments whose historical significance is overlaid by the fame of *being famous*. When we visit it in Athens or in the British Museum, we are not only searching out a masterpiece of classical Greece; there are, after all, a good number of classical temples bigger or better preserved than this that never attract such attention. We are also following in the footsteps of all those who have visited before (that's why we want *our* photographs taken there too …); and we are paying tribute to a symbol that has been written into our own cultural history, from Keats, through Freud to Nashville. But, in the case of the Parthenon, there is yet another dimension. We are visiting a monument that has been fought over for generations, that enflames passions and prompts government intervention. It has the added distinction, in other words, of being *worth arguing about*. The uncomfortable conclusion is hard to resist: that, if it had not been dismembered, the Parthenon would never have been half so famous.

··

2

'THE TEMPLE THEY CALL THE
PARTHENON'

A GUIDE IN HAND

Only one brief description of the Parthenon survives from the ancient world itself. It runs to a single paragraph in a *Guidebook to Greece* written by an enthusiastic traveller in the mid-second century AD, almost 600 years after the monument was built. In striking contrast to the flood of modern eulogies, Greek and Roman writers remained remarkably reticent on the Parthenon. True, they were probably not so reticent as they now appear. An enormous amount of classical literature has been lost over the centuries; in fact, almost anything that medieval scribes or their patrons did not choose to copy has not survived – it is as simple, and chancy, as that. Victims of this neglect certainly include a technical treatise by one of the building's architects, Iktinos, and at least two multi-volume gazetteers to the Athenian Acropolis which must have featured the temple prominently. As it is, for the ancient view of the Parthenon we now rely on the description of a writer called Pausanias, a Greek speaker from the western seaboard of what is now Turkey, writing more or less the ancient equivalent of a *Blue Guide*. He toured Greece when the country had long since become a comfortable, demilitarised province of the Roman empire – even if there were still bitter memories of the brutal conquest by the Romans in the second century BC. By his day Athens was a slightly self-satisfied university town and a notable highspot in the ancient 'heritage trail'; its monuments were tourist attractions almost as much as they are today.

Unlike Freud, Pausanias made a beeline for the Athenian Acropolis. The first of his 10 volumes opens with the account of his arrival on the coast near Athens, sailing past the sanctuary at Sounion where Byron was later to carve his name. Once through the city gates, there were any number of attractions to engage and detain him: statues by the most illustrious Greek artists; celebrity tombs; historic government buildings; ancient sanctuaries; paintings of notable Athenian victories from their glory days before the Romans (or, for that matter, before Philip of Macedon effectively stamped out Athenian independence in the fourth century BC). But by the middle of the book he was all set to take his readers up the single road, 'precipitous throughout', leading to the Acropolis (*Figure 3*).

This was not the bare rock that it is now, with just a few isolated monuments dramatically silhouetted against a clear sky. It was the most important sacred space in the whole of Athens, as well as the prime site of civic memory and display. As such, it was crammed with statues, shrines and curiosities, many of which Pausanias stops to describe, explaining their origin and elaborating their history with a whole range of more or less curious myths and stories. One minute it is the legend of Theseus' father who plunged to his death just where the little temple of the goddess Victory later stood. The next minute he is pointing to a group of Graces and explaining how 'everyone says' that it was sculpted by Socrates, the greatest guru-philosopher of the fifth century BC (a nice idea ... but we now think that it was much more likely the work of a second-division sculptor from Thebes, also called Socrates). One minute he is floored by the sheer quantity of works of art to describe, and warns us that he will not even be mentioning some of the less distinguished pieces. The next he is fussing over a small stone where, once upon a time, Silenus, one of the rowdy friends of the god Dionysus, was said to have stopped for a rest. And so the sights and stories flood out.

When he finally reaches 'the temple they call the Parthenon', the account is almost uncomfortably low-key. There is no gush of admiration, not a single superlative. He starts with a brief glance at the scenes depicted in the two temple gables: 'as you go in, all the sculpture in the so-called "pediment" is about the birth of Athena; the subject of the pediment at the back of the building is the contest between Poseidon and Athena for the territory of Athens'. He finishes with a note of the only two portrait statues he claims to remember seeing there. The first is of Hadrian, Roman emperor and fanatical admirer of Greek culture, who poured money into a magnificent facelift for Athens in the early second century AD (including, if you were to believe Payne Knight, the Parthenon sculptures themselves). The other, 'by the door', is a statue of Iphicrates, a fourth-century BC general-cum-mercenary who, as Pausanias rather vaguely writes, 'did many amazing things'. His memory sometimes served him better. Elsewhere in his *Guidebook* he brings up a painting in the Parthenon which featured the fifth-century BC general (later defector and exile) Themistocles, as well as

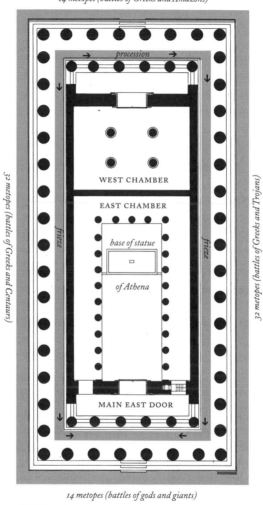

Contest between Athena and Poseidon

14 metopes (battles of Greeks and Amazons)

procession

WEST CHAMBER

EAST CHAMBER

base of statue

of Athena

MAIN EAST DOOR

frieze

frieze

32 metopes (battles of Greeks and Centaurs)

32 metopes (battles of Greeks and Trojans)

14 metopes (battles of gods and giants)

Birth of Athena

Figure 2. The Parthenon and its sculpture (scale 1:400).

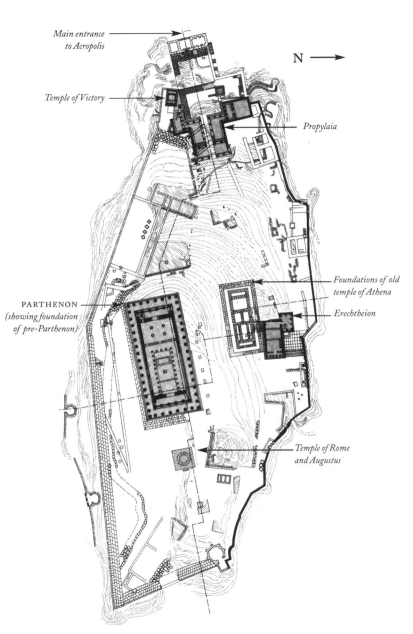

Main entrance to Acropolis

Temple of Victory

Propylaia

N ⟶

Foundations of old temple of Athena

Erechtheion

PARTHENON
(showing foundation of pre-Parthenon)

Temple of Rome and Augustus

Figure 3. Plan of the ancient Acropolis.

a portrait of someone called Heliodorus, whose tomb he passed on the way to Eleusis. But his mind is not on those here.

For, in the rest of his account, some 20 lines or so in all, Pausanias has eyes for one object only: the virtuoso statue, now lost without trace, of the goddess Athena which took pride of place inside the building. She was made of ivory and gold, he explains, and stood up straight, dressed in a tunic that stretched to her feet. On her head she wore an elaborate helmet, with a sphinx in the centre and griffins on either side; while her breastplate carried as its emblem the face and snaky locks (here worked in ivory) of one of her celebrated victims. This was the gorgon Medusa who, so the story went, had turned to stone anyone unlucky enough to catch sight of her – until the goddess helped a plucky young hero to do the necessary and decapitate the monster. The whole statue was set on a pedestal which was itself decorated with sculpture showing the creation of the first mortal woman, Pandora. Pausanias lingers here: 'before Pandora came into being', he insists, 'there was as yet no race of women'. It was indeed a turning point in the history of mankind, for Pandora was a treacherous gift made by the gods as a punishment for men's disobedience and, not unlike Eve, the origin of all human trouble.

Athena was also equipped with a number of her characteristic props. In one hand she grasped a spear. In the other she held a statue of the goddess Victory; this alone, Pausanias says, was 'four cubits' tall. Finally, at her side lay a shield and a serpent, 'presumably Erichthonios'. He expects his readers to know that 'Erichthonios' was the son of the virgin goddess, by a miraculous conception that lay at the heart of local legend. Athena had gone one day, they said, to the god Hephaistos, the divine blacksmith, to kit herself out with a new set of weapons. But he had other things on his mind, namely sex. The predictable tussle ensued. Athena sternly fended him off and Hephaistos only got close enough to ejaculate over her leg. Divine seed, though, was powerful stuff. When Athena cleaned herself up and brushed it to the ground, up popped Erichthonios – either, as some versions of the myth held, in the shape of a serpent, or as a more recognisably human baby – who would grow up to be one of the founding fathers of the city of Athens.

Brief as it is, Pausanias' account is absolutely crucial in helping us to picture the ancient Parthenon. Without it, we would have very little clue what any of the battered pieces of sculpture that survive from the pediments could possibly have been meant to be. It still remains a puzzle, as we shall see, how exactly the group over the main entrance captured in marble the birth of Athena, who, in another divine twist of the normal mechanisms of human reproduction, was supposed to have emerged fully formed and fully armed from the head of her father Zeus. There are some doubts too, at the other end of the building, about how the sculptors managed to depict what Pausanias calls the 'contest between Poseidon and Athena': the legendary auction, in which the two deities offered rival bids for control of the city of Athens, Athena's olive tree winning out against Poseidon's offer of the sea. And, of course, he may not have understood these scenes in exactly the same way as other visitors did, let alone as their artists had envisaged them. (Indeed, on a few notable occasions elsewhere in his *Guidebook*, modern commentators have decided that his descriptions must be, in detail, quite wrong.)

Nevertheless, Pausanias offers a first-hand, eye-witness interpretation to get us going. He is the starting point too when we try to imagine the phenomenal statue of Athena. This was made of gold and ivory – not, of course, solid but a precious covering over a wooden frame (in fact, classical writers joked about the mice that lived in the hollow interiors of statues such as this). Frankly, to modern ears, Pausanias' account makes it sound an appallingly vulgar confection, an uncomfortable mixture of materials, overblown and overloaded, about as far from 'the classical ideal' as you could get; and this impression is horribly confirmed by every modern attempt to reconstruct the object (*Illustration 3*). But, like it or not, Athena must have been the star attraction of the temple.

Paradoxically, though, what Pausanias leaves out of his account of the Parthenon has attracted almost as much attention as what he includes. He may go to town on the statue of Athena, but he spares not a word for the architecture that has been so eulogised by more recent visitors; nor does he stop to mention the names of the architects or sculptors involved. Even more disconcerting for most modern students of classical art, he says nothing at all about the metope panels or the sculpted frieze that ran round the whole building. The frieze, in particular, has become for us the touchstone of classical art, its 'calm and understated beauty' (as one recent book has it) standing for all we love – or hate – about Greek art in the fifth century BC. So why does Pausanias say nothing? Did he just fail to notice it? If so, was it because he was generally unobservant or simply tired and losing concentration by the time he reached the Parthenon? Or was it that the frieze was actually very difficult to see? High up on the wall, behind an outer colonnade, maybe it was effectively hidden from even the most conscientious ancient tourist. Or is it because it came low on his list of priorities, so far below the statue of Athena that it did not rate even a word? Any of these alternatives is possible. But whichever we choose (and, for my money, the last seems the most likely – and would explain his silence about the very visible metope panels as well), it should remind us just how difficult it is to reconstruct the way in which any ancient viewer saw the Parthenon, or what they made of what they saw.

DRESSING UP ATHENS LIKE A WHORE

A few of the gaps left by Pausanias can be filled by another account, written some decades earlier, also by a Greek living under the Roman empire – the hugely learned and prolific Plutarch. Writing around the turn of the first and second centuries AD, Plutarch was responsible for a whole library of essays, ranging from technical treatises on whether water animals are more intelligent than land animals to more practical advice on what makes a marriage work. But since the sixteenth century (when, via a best-selling English translation, he provided Shakespeare with most of the historical colour for his *Julius Caesar*, *Antony and Cleopatra* and *Coriolanus*), he has been best known for his biographies, more than 40 surviving life-stories of distinguished Greeks and Romans. These include the *Life of Pericles*, the Athenian aristocrat, democratic ideologue, general and ultimately warmonger, who was the prime mover in getting the Parthenon project off the ground in the 440s BC.

Pericles is a puzzling figure. He was, without doubt, a

brilliant vote-catching politician. Repeatedly elected 'general' by the Athenian people in the mid-fifth century BC (technically a military post, but with much wider influence), he dominated the political process, some would argue, in a way that sat uneasily next to his democratic credentials. He was also given a magnificent and hugely influential write-up by Thucydides, the fifth-century historian who charted the Great War between Athens and Sparta in the final decades of the century. Early in his *History* Thucydides puts into Pericles' mouth a tear-jerking speech (supposedly delivered at the state funeral for the brave warriors who had died in the first year of the war) which has often been read as a powerful manifesto for Athenian democratic culture. 'We are called a democracy because Athens is run with the interests of the majority in mind … we are lovers of beauty yet without extravagance and lovers of wisdom without being soft … our city as a whole is an education for Greece.' It is heady stuff, which has been conscripted in support of all kinds of 'civilised values' ever since (and was, in fact, plastered over London buses during the First World War).

But this is only one side of Pericles. Some of the others are, for us, considerably less palatable. Like many superpowers since, Athens saw no contradiction between democratic freedom at home and aggressive imperialism overseas. Pericles' hawkish influence almost certainly lay behind the increasingly ruthless treatment meted out to Athens' overseas 'allies' in the course of the century. One particularly lurid anecdote tells of Pericles ordering the crucifixion of the leaders of the breakaway island of Samos; when the unfortunate rebels were still alive 10 days later, he had their heads clubbed in and their bodies thrown out without burial. Or so, at least, one Samian patriot was to claim a century and a half later. Pericles was also one of the prime movers in provoking the city of Sparta to war – a war that Athens would so disastrously lose, ending up in 404 BC with a catastrophic casualty list, democracy suspended and a murderous (if short-lived) Spartan-backed junta in control.

Plutarch saw things rather differently; indeed he made a point of denying the truth of the grisly story about the crucifixions. Writing more than half a millennium after Pericles' death, when fifth-century BC Athens had long since become an almost mythical time of past glory, he had no doubts about his hero's wisdom, probity and military expertise. He enthused in particular over what was to be Pericles' most enduring achievement – namely, the vast schemes for new building that he initiated in and around Athens. As Plutarch ruefully reflects, this was about the only clear evidence that remained in his day to prove that Greece really had once been rich and powerful.

The 'Periclean building programme', as modern historians tend to call it, involved much more than the construction of the Parthenon, significant as that may have been. For it was only part of a radical makeover for the Acropolis as a whole. This included the grand Propylaia, or monumental gateway, which was singled out by Thucydides as the flagship building of the site and was on any estimate not much less expensive than the Parthenon itself, as well as a brand new Odeion, or 'Music Hall', on the hill-slopes (it was here that Athenian dramatists gave previews of their plays, and comic writers joked that its shape was very like that of Pericles' own head). Also in the scheme for the Acropolis was a new sanctuary of the goddess Artemis between the Parthenon and the

Propylaia; plus two smaller temples, one to Athena (the so-called Erechtheion, with its famous line-up of female columns or caryatids), the other to Victory (Athena Nike), both of which were completed after Pericles' death in 429 BC. Further afield, Pericles was also behind a revamped Hall of the Mysteries for the ancient sanctuary of Demeter at Eleusis, as well as a variety of rather more mundane projects for well-houses, defensive walls and gymnasia.

More systematically than Pausanias, Plutarch names names, conjuring up an elite circle of artists and architects hard at work to realise Pericles' vision for Athens: the designers of the Parthenon, Iktinos and Kallicrates; Mnesikles, who was in charge of the Propylaia; Koroibos, who died too soon to see his Hall of the Mysteries completed; but, above all, the sculptor Pheidias, who was responsible for the gold and ivory creation inside the Parthenon, as well as acting as designer, site-manager and general overseer of the whole programme. If we were to follow Plutarch, we would see the partnership of Pericles and Pheidias as one of those brilliant combinations of politician-patron and artistic genius: Pheidias playing Michelangelo to Pericles' Pope Julius II (or, let's face it, Speer to Pericles' Hitler).

Plutarch painted a vivid picture of the impact of the building works on Athens and its citizens: whole armies of specialist craftsmen – carpenters, sculptors, engravers, bronzesmiths, painters, gilders – were enlisted; so too were vast numbers of tradesmen, suppliers, miners and hauliers who came up with the raw materials and delivered them to the different sites. Almost everyone in the city had some part to play: ropemakers and roadbuilders were needed as never before. Meanwhile, the master artists pulled out all the stops to produce their very best, but never once missed the contract's deadline. Plutarch must have been as familiar as we are with projects not finished on time and it was the amazing promptness of the programme that impressed him more than anything else. 'The most wondrous thing of all', he wrote, 'was the speed of their work,' and he pondered quizzically on the paradox that monuments which were to last for all time were constructed in almost no time at all. They appeared old and venerable from the moment they were built, he went on, yet they seemed fresh and new, 'untouched by time', even 500 years later.

All the same, Pericles' plans were not universally popular. Plutarch counted it to his hero's credit that he had managed to overcome carping critics of the wonderful building programme. But clearly a strong tradition existed in Plutarch's day (and some of it at least will have gone back to the fifth century BC) that the Parthenon and the other monuments sponsored by Pericles had been intensely controversial from the very beginning. Some of the criticisms, as reported, sound like the usual stories of sex and peculation that often cluster around great architectural schemes. Pheidias, for example, was accused of fiddling the books by skimping on the gold used on the great statue of Athena in the Parthenon; according to Plutarch it was all carefully removed and weighed, and Pheidias was (of course) completely exonerated. Others suggested that Pericles was using his site-meetings with Pheidias as a cover for secret assignations with attractive female art-lovers, conveniently procured by the great sculptor himself. There was also a nasty scandal about some of the images that decorated the outside of Athena's shield. The overall design was part of the standard repertoire of classical temple art and, in itself, entirely uncontroversial: scenes of valiant Greeks battling against the mythical warrior-race of women, the Amazons. But among the legendary Greek fighters, people claimed to recognise two real-life portraits: 'a figure something like Pheidias himself as a bald old man lifting up a rock in both hands and a very beautiful image of Pericles fighting an Amazon'. Sacrilege, or merely a case of ill-judged self-promotion? Whatever the exact charge, Plutarch claimed that Pheidias was hauled off to prison – where, mastermind of the Parthenon or not, he languished and soon died. Other evidence, however, suggests a happier outcome. Certainly, if we were to believe Plutarch, we would find it hard to explain how we hear of the same Pheidias a few years later, putting his stamp on another vast gold and ivory creation – this time the statue of Zeus in the sanctuary at Olympia.

But Plutarch also suggests that in the mid-fifth century BC there were more strident, political, objections to the whole Parthenon project. Pericles' rivals attacked the building works as a colossal waste of money and (even more to the point) as an insult to the Athenians' 'allies', whose contributions to a common defence budget were being squandered on titivating the city of Athens. Plutarch puts some tough talking into the mouth of this opposition. 'Greece must obviously think she is being terribly insulted and tyrannised, when she sees the tribute we have taken from her by force for the war used to gild and prettify our city like some vain woman, bedecking itself with expensive stones and statues and temples worth millions.' Almost certainly these exact words are an invention of Plutarch himself, wheeled out specifically to be trounced by some even tougher talking on the part of Pericles. None the less, the charge of 'dressing up Athens like a whore' (as an alternative translation puts it), out of the dubious profits of empire, is one that still hovers over the whole Parthenon scheme.

The roots of this accusation go back decades before any of the building plans had even begun to take shape. In fact, they go back to the early fifth century BC and to the single most significant event in the forging of classical Greek identity: the war between the Greeks and the vast Persian empire, a conflict which ended in 479 BC with a glorious, if costly, Greek victory. This war had an enormous influence over the history of the next 100 years or more, and over almost every aspect of the Parthenon, including (as we shall see later) its decorative scheme. As with all the most memorable victories, the Greek success was against the odds. On the Persian side it was a revenge match. There had been an earlier dent to Persian pride in 490, when they raided Greece with (for them) a relatively modest force and the Athenians, as they never ceased to boast, pulled off a tremendous massacre at the battle of Marathon. In 480, the invaders came back again with their full battalions, numbering – according to the ludicrously patriotic exaggeration of the Greek historian Herodotus – more than 5 million troops; but certainly enough to outnumber the Greek forces heavily, even at the more sober modern guesses of some 650,000.

The unexpected Greek victory can be put down to the simple fact that, for once, most of the wilfully separatist cities of Greece (or 'fiercely independent', to use the usual euphemism) pulled together; the threat from Persia, temporarily at least, called a halt to their usual hostilities. Significant too was the Greek readiness to sustain terrible losses in the cause of ultimate success. Three hundred heroic – or brainwashed – Spartans effectively committed suicide trying to block the Persian advance through the pass at Thermopylae (William Golding, in mellower mood than in front of the Parthenon, saw the Spartan commander here as a martyr in the cause of freedom against oriental despotism, Persian-style: 'A little of Leonidas lies in the fact that I can go where I like and write what I like. He contributed to set us free ...'). Meanwhile, Athens itself was evacuated and the Persians, albeit on their way to defeat, had the satisfaction of destroying the town, looting and burning the temples and other monuments that then stood on the Acropolis.

But how long would the victory last? When the Persians scuttled back home in 479, most Greeks must have assumed that sooner or later they would be back. To keep their defences ready, a group of Greek cities, large and small, clubbed together in a loose military alliance; more than 200 of them were involved in the middle of the century, but at the beginning they probably numbered fewer than 100. Athens was at the head and provided the organisation and strategic command; each of the member states made a contribution, either in cash or in war ships plus crew; the fighting fund and financial reserves were kept on the island of Delos (hence the alliance's modern title, the Delian League). Over the next 25 years or so, there was a series of sporadic encounters with Persian forces, including a thundering Greek victory over the Persian fleet on the river Eurymedon (in modern Turkey), and an equally thundering Greek defeat in Egypt. But, even so, there was nothing on the scale that the allies most likely predicted.

In fact, before long some League members began to feel

more anxious about Athenian ambitions than about any menace from Persia. For the hawks at Athens were busy turning an alliance of independent cities into a ruthlessly controlled empire. A decisive turning point came in 454 when the Treasury was transferred from Delos to Athens – the financial reserves ending up, appropriately enough, inside the Parthenon when it was completed. From this point too, any joint meetings of the League ceased and all decisions were in the hands of the Athenians. But some member cities clearly resented Athens' grip much earlier: from the 470s on, although new cities were still coming into the League, others were attempting to jump ship and to stop payment of what was now, in effect, imperial tribute. Mostly with disastrous consequences. Defectors were brought back by force and made to see the error of their ways. Garrisons and governors, the destruction of a city's defences and the insistence that capital crimes were tried in Athens itself under Athenian law (a neat way of protecting Athens' friends in allied cities from judicial execution), were just a few of the weapons in the armoury of Athenian control.

The building and the funding of the Parthenon are insep-arable from the Athenian empire, its profits, its debates and discontents. Plutarch's general picture of Athens in the 440s may be misleading in all kinds of ways. The impression he gives, for example, of a highly planned, centrally directed programme of public works, with major artists at the beck and call of the powers that be, probably owes more to his experience of the vast urban redevelopments sponsored by Roman emperors than to any knowledge of what actually went on in the fifth century BC. And his emphasis on full employment for the masses fails to acknowledge the simple fact that much of the labour (and certainly all the roughest work) would have been carried out by slaves. None the less, his account is an important reminder of the controversies that must have surrounded the Parthenon from the moment it was first mooted. A glorious celebration of Athens, maybe. But, for at least a minority of Athenians, it could equally well have stood for the misuse of the profits of their empire. As for the 'allies', even if some of them were proud at the way their money had been spent (all empires, we should remember, are popular with some of their subjects), others could only have seen the Parthenon as a powerful symbol of their humiliation.

THE BARE ESSENTIALS

We know just the barest essentials about the Parthenon as the Greeks and Romans saw it. Apart from the remains themselves (tricky as we shall find them to interpret), and what we learn from Pausanias and Plutarch, the evidence is tantalisingly elusive. There is a clutch of brief references and passing allusions in other classical writers: Plutarch's biography of Demetrios Poliorketes, for example, describes how this fourth-century BC warlord took up residence there (with permission) – 'and Athena was said to entertain him and act as his host, even though he was a dreadfully disorderly guest and did not treat his lodging with the *politesse* due to a virgin'. Predictably perhaps, the vast statue of the goddess claims most of what attention there is. The omnivorous Roman polymath Pliny spares it several lines in his roster of famous sculpture, noting its total height, 26 cubits, and how it was crammed with decoration on the shield and even the sandals (which were themselves, according to a second-century AD Greek lexicographer, 'of Etruscan type'). While in his satiric comedy *The Knights*, first staged in the middle of the Great War between Athens and Sparta (when Pheidias' creation was little more than a decade old), Aristophanes bandies a joke about cakes made by the enormous 'ivory hand' of Athena herself.

From all the evidence combined, we know enough about this lost statue to be able to identify a whole variety of smaller scale versions found all over the ancient world in marble, bronze and terracotta, as well as on coins and gems. The latest count gives a total of more than 200, not including the coins: they range from what must be reasonably careful 'copies' of Pheidias' original to imaginative echoes of the famous masterpiece; from works at roughly half the original size to miniatures no more than a centimetre tall; from gold pendants laid to rest with a rich lady in the Crimea in the early fourth century BC, featuring the statue's head (in an almost exact match of Pausanias' description), to a chunky, marble, three-and-a-half metre adaptation commissioned for the reading room of the royal library at Pergamon, in modern Turkey, in the second century BC. Whatever impetus lies behind these versions – piety, love of art, the souvenir trade or (in the case of the brash new dynasty at Pergamon) a desire to cash in on the cultural capital of Athens – taken together they attest the impact, right across the ancient world, of the Parthenon's centrepiece, far beyond what we would ever guess from surviving ancient literature.

From Athens itself another small cache of material gives us a glimpse of the ancient Parthenon, from an unexpected angle. One of the obsessions of the classical Athenian democracy was public accountability. In pursuit of openness and transparency in government, they put on public display the records of all kinds of official decisions and financial transactions, laboriously inscribed on stone, 'for anyone who wanted to see' (how many of the intended audience in fifth-century Athens could actually read, even supposing they were interested in this arid bureaucratese, is quite another matter). Among the many thousands of such inscribed documents that survive, there are a few that refer to the Parthenon. We shall look in Chapter 5 at the inscribed inventories of its contents: for the Athenians, these were a weapon in the fight against embezzlement and theft; for us, they are a rare hint of the precious bric-à-brac that once cluttered the inside of the temple, from Persian daggers and broken stools to gold cups and ivory lyres.

Just as revealing is a small group of fragments from the inscribed accounts for the building work itself and for the production of the statue of Athena. What remains amounts to less than 10 per cent of the original text, and there is still a good deal of dispute about how, or where, some of the smaller pieces should be fitted into the whole picture. The ingenuity with which scholars have reconstructed what was written on the missing sections is often hard to distinguish from sheer fantasy. All the same, enough survives to allow us to fix the exact dates of the construction on site – starting in 447/6 BC (the Athenian year ran from summer solstice to summer solstice) and completed in 433/2. And in some places we can deduce the order in which the work was carried out. The first year, for example, includes payment for quarrying and transporting marble (presumably the start of the enormous task of extracting the marble from the quarries on

Mount Pentelicon and carting it the 18 kilometres to Athens). The payment for wood in 444/3 has been thought to indicate scaffolding. The selling off of spare gold in 438/7 is a strong hint that the gold and ivory statue was by then finished.

There is much more, however, that we simply do not know about the ancient Parthenon. This is not only a question of bad luck – the unfortunate disappearance of just those ancient texts that might have answered our most burning questions, or the random destruction of those parts of the building we would so much like to have survived. Of course, it is in part that. We would almost certainly be in a much better position to understand the Parthenon if the Ottoman Turks had not used it as an ammunition store and so made it an irresistible target for their Venetian enemies to attack in 1687 – causing, as we shall see in the next chapter, enormous damage to the structure and sculpture. But other things are at issue too, much more fundamental to our understanding of the classical past as a whole. For to study the Parthenon is to be brought face to face with the very fragility of our grip on the Greek and Roman world, and with the challenges (or frustrations, depending on your mood) that are involved in even the simplest attempts to describe it, let alone explain or make sense of it. The Parthenon, in other words, offers an object lesson in those tantalising processes of investigation, deduction, empathy, reconstruction and sheer guesswork that must be the hallmarks of any study of classics and the classical past.

Our dilemmas start with the name of the building. The Greeks gave it various titles. The most usual was probably the *hekatompedon* or '100-footer', perhaps after the exact dimensions of some part of the building, or perhaps just indicating 'big'. But we, like Pausanias and his informants, 'call it the Parthenon'. But why? One common guess is that it was originally the name of one of the inner rooms, and only later applied to the building as a whole; but we cannot be sure. The Greek word *parthenos* means 'virgin', and Parthenos was indeed one of the titles given to the virgin goddess Athena. But modern scholars have found it hard to decide whether it was the goddess who gave the title to the temple, or the temple to the goddess. To complicate things further, the word Parthenon in its Greek form (the last syllable is spelled with a long o, or omega – Parthen-*oh*-n) does not mean 'virgin'; but more precisely 'of the virgins', in the plural. This has prompted a whole range of desperate speculations about the use of part of the temple for housing a group of pre-pubescent girls employed in weaving the sacred textiles used in the worship of Athena (making it literally a 'house – or room – of the virgins').

Many other basic questions also remain the subject of lively debate. No one can agree, for example, how the sculptural decoration was painted. It is one thing to accept (as most people now do) that some kind of colour was applied to the marble, that it was not the pure brilliant white that, since the Renaissance, we have come to expect of classical statuary. But are we dealing with a discreet background wash to reduce the glare of the marble, plus the careful highlighting of certain crucial details? Or was it a garish confection of bright reds, yellows and blues, about as distant as it is possible to imagine from that 'calm and understated beauty' that is supposed to characterise classical art? Not even the resources of modern scientific analysis directed to the surviving traces of 'paint' on the marble provide a clear answer. And there is even more controversy about what much of the sculpture (garish or not) was meant to represent. The famous frieze is well preserved, and has been minutely studied for 200 years. Yet there is little consensus about what it is trying to show, beyond a solemn procession of some sort. Does it, for example, feature the men and women of fifth-century BC Athens engaged in some real-life Athenian ritual? Or is it, as one influential recent theory holds, a preparation for human sacrifice, drawn from the repertoire of local Athenian myth? We have no ancient text to help us out. How on earth are we supposed to decide between all the different 'solutions'?

Even more to the point, perhaps, what was the building as a whole *for*? The obvious answer that it was a 'temple' (and so essentially 'religious') is not quite so obvious as it might seem. There were no priests or priestesses attached to the Parthenon, no ancient religious festival or ritual is known to have taken place there, and it did not even have that most basic piece of Greek temple equipment: an altar directly outside its front entrance. Faced with these difficulties, some scholars have tried to argue that, despite all appearances, it was not actually a 'temple' at all. Instead, they suggest, we should think of the Parthenon as a particularly grand treasury (for it certainly housed most of Athens' accumulated reserves), or as a spectacular thank-offering to the goddess for her help in defeating the Persians. Others have resisted. After all, 'temple' is exactly what Pausanias calls it. Maybe it would be better, they argue, to think more carefully about what we expect of an ancient temple, and how we would decide what counted as one and what did not.

There are all kinds of wider historical issues at stake too.

Why, for example, was the building work started when it was? The Persians had destroyed the earlier monuments on the Acropolis in 480 BC. So why wait more than 30 years before embarking on a restoration programme? Some ancient writers, presumably with this same question in mind, referred to a solemn oath sworn by the Greeks in 479 just before their final victory, forbidding any such thing: 'I will rebuild none of the temples that have been burned and cast down, but I will leave them as a monument to men hereafter, a memorial of the impiety of the barbarians'. But, if this pro-hibition really was in force (and already by the fourth century BC, cynics could dismiss the idea of such an oath as a piece of self-serving fiction), why was rebuilding suddenly allowed in the 440s? Certainly the sharpest memories of the Persians will have dulled somewhat by then – and the ruins on the Acropolis might well have come to seem more of a nuisance than a poignant memorial. But was the oath just conven-iently forgotten? Or was it made irrelevant, as later Greek tradition had it, by a formal peace treaty between Greeks and Persia – which would also have removed the original *raison d'être* of the Delian League?

And who paid? The final price-tag on the Parthenon is utterly elusive. Most modern estimates reckon that the building itself cost less than the gold and ivory statue. But the exact figures produced – based on the fragments of sur-viving accounts, on what we know of the price of raw ma-terials, transport and labour in the ancient world, plus inevitably a good deal of guesswork – vary by a factor of more than four. On the most modest, the whole building seems a bargain, not even reaching the total given by Thucydides for Athens' annual income from the empire just before the start of the Great War. On the largest, it becomes an enormous drain on resources, and the whole Periclean building programme looks like a ghastly financial folly. But whichever figure you choose (or wherever on the spectrum in between), there is still the question of how far Plutarch's objectors had a point. Did the allied budget really foot the bulk of the bill for 'dressing up Athens like a whore'? Not surprisingly, modern opinion is divided here too. The majority view is that the fragmentary inscriptions of the building accounts do indeed confirm that huge transfers were made from the fighting fund to the building programme. But recently others have concluded, on the basis of exactly the same evidence, of course, that relatively little of the allies' money was used; no more, in fact, than the tiny percentage of their contributions which was given as a regular offering each year to Athena herself (and could, you might argue, perfectly legitimately be used in building her a brand-new temple). But, in this case, maybe the difference does not matter so very much. However the bookkeeping was done, and however much the various pockets of finance were kept (formally) separate, the wealth of Athens in the mid-fifth century BC was both a direct and indirect consequence of its empire – and it was that empire that paid for the Parthenon.

In the chapters that follow I shall be scratching the surface of a number of these controversies, and thinking harder about how we can make sense of the ancient Parthenon and the culture in which it was created. But at the same time I shall constantly be keeping an eye on its later history, after antiquity and up to the present day. The Parthenon is, after all, as much a modern icon as an ancient ruin. If we wish to understand its significance in the ancient world, we need also to understand what has happened to it over the last two millennia, and how we have come to invest in it so much of our own cultural energy. It is for this reason that Chapter 3 starts in the Middle Ages.

3

....

'THE FINEST MOSQUE
IN THE WORLD'

In 1175, or thereabouts, Michael Choniates, a scholarly priest with an influential desk-job in Constantinople, left home to become Archbishop of Athens. Greece was then an unpromising backwater of the Byzantine empire, the Christian descendant of the Roman empire in the eastern Mediterranean. And Athens itself was little more than a large village of just a few thousand inhabitants (most of them living on or near the Acropolis), and no match for its neighbours, Thebes and Corinth, both of which had found a lucrative opening in producing silk for the grandees of the imperial capital at Constantinople. Athens was left trading instead on the allure of its distinguished classical past. This was an increasingly difficult act to sustain, but from time to time the old magic still worked – as it did, to start with at least, for Michael Choniates.

We still have the text of the inaugural sermon he preached to his flock in his new cathedral. It was a brilliant piece of would-be classical rhetoric. Learned allusions to ancient literature jostled with pointed references to Pericles and the victorious warriors of the battle of Marathon, as Michael piled on the compliments about Athens' historic greatness. 'She was the queen of cities,' he proclaimed, 'nurse of reason and virtue … exalted in fame not just for the monuments, but for virtue and wisdom of every description.' The Athenians of his own day were, he argued, of exactly the same mettle, but with a crucial advantage: they were Christians and worshipped the one true God. No longer did that false virgin Athena, the mother of Erichthonios, captivate the city – but the one and only, eternal Virgin Mary. The sermon must have lasted a good hour, if he delivered the whole of the text that we now have. In his final rhetorical flourish he pumped up the emotion even further, casting Athens as the peak of heaven itself, the new Mount Horeb ('though I must be careful not to think I'm Moses', he joked with the congregation). Such was the power of Christian truth and classical culture combined.

The sermon was not the success he had hoped. Michael had crafted a speech that might well have charmed a select audience in the fifth century BC, and would almost certainly have gone down well in clerical circles in his own Constantinople. But the backwoods congregation of twelfth-century Athens did not relish all those smart allusions to ancient literature and the more remote corners of classical myth and history (how many of them, can we imagine, would have ever heard of Erichthonios?). It all went way over their heads. In a sermon delivered shortly after, he accused his benighted flock of simply not understanding him: 'My inaugural address was perfectly plain and straightforward, but what I was saying was apparently unintelligible; I might as well have been speaking Persian or Scythian.' On other occasions, he complained of the Athenians' utter ignorance of their own heroic past, their horrible dialect and the way they chattered and shuffled their feet in church – not to mention their nasty wine ('pressed from resinous pines rather than clusters of grapes') and hopeless backwardness (not a metal-worker or a wheelwright amongst them). We should not take all of this literally, and imagine an utterly poverty-stricken community. The notion that the 'modern' Athenians were not a patch on their classical predecessors is itself a cliché that goes back at least to the third century BC. And, no matter what he thought of their cultural attainments, Michael proved a sturdy defender of the interests of his flock – particularly in the face of pressing tax-collectors and the high-handed demands of the imperial governor. All the same, the town turned out to be a far cry from the heaven he had imagined in his first sermon.

The one thing in Athens that did not disappoint him was his wonderful cathedral, where he preached that first sermon. He praised it repeatedly – it was light and airy, quite simply 'lovely'; and he referred enthusiastically to some of its renowned adornments. There was, for example, a miraculous lamp that burned continuously, its oil never failing. And he singled out as a highlight the golden dove, with a golden crown, that hung down over the altar, circling continuously around the cross – a symbol of the Holy Spirit. His cathedral was, of course, what we would call the Parthenon, now adapted to Christian use and dedicated to the Virgin (Mary), Our Lady of Athens. It is an uncomfortable truth for devotees of classical culture that the only ceremony ever to have taken place in the monument that we can document in any detail is no spectacular ritual from the glory days of the Athenian empire in the fifth century BC; it is this inauguration of a Byzantine archbishop, centuries into the Middle Ages.

Classical temples made good churches on a grand scale. They were relatively easy, and cheap, for the early Christians to adapt; and there must have been a certain satisfaction in converting pagan monuments to the glory of the 'true God'. Archaeologists see these adaptations as a godsend in a quite different sense; for it is Christian re-use that has regularly guaranteed the preservation of the original structure. Left unoccupied, ancient temples fall down – aided, as often as not, by later builders scavenging for materials. As a rule of thumb, temples that still stand to their full height, roof and all, owe their survival to the early Christians. You can walk inside the ancient Pantheon in Rome, even now, thanks to those who consecrated it to St Mary of the Martyrs in AD 608; and, only a short walk from the Acropolis, the so-called Theseum in Athens (in fact, not a temple of Theseus at all, but of the god Hephaistos) escaped destruction in the guise of a church of St George. Had it not been for the catastrophic explosion of 1687, there is a strong chance that the Parthenon too would have survived largely complete, under the protection of its new name and function.

We do not know the exact date at which the Parthenon ceased to be a pagan temple, or (for it was not necessarily a seamless transition) when it became a church. A whole series of decrees outlawing pagan worship were issued by Roman, then Byzantine, emperors from the fourth century AD on. But the traditional religion of the Greek world held out much more valiantly than most Christian writers cared to admit. Currently the best guess for the date of the temple's conversion to Christian use is sometime in the sixth century. Not many structural changes to the building were needed;

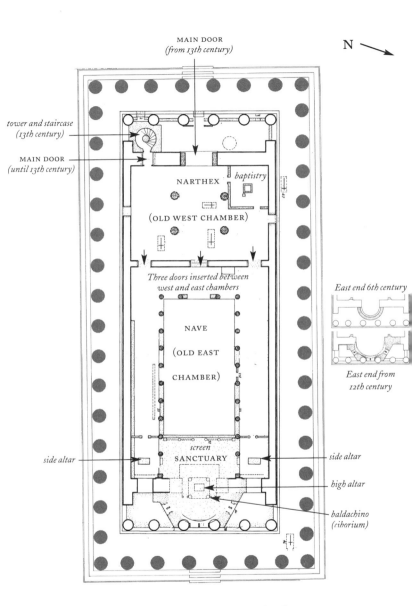

MAIN DOOR
(from 13th century)

N

tower and staircase
(13th century)

MAIN DOOR
(until 13th century)

NARTHEX   *baptistry*

(OLD WEST CHAMBER)

Three doors inserted between
west and east chambers

NAVE

(OLD EAST

CHAMBER)

East end 6th century

East end from
12th century

screen
SANCTUARY

side altar   *side altar*

high altar

baldachino
(ciborium)

Figure 4. The Parthenon as a church.

though its orientation did have to be reversed (*Figure 4*). The classical temple had its main entrance at the east, under the sculpture in the pediment that depicted the birth of the goddess herself. It was at this end that the Christians wanted their altar. So they blocked up the east doorway with an apse, expertly recycled (or opportunistically thrown together, depending on your point of view) from fragments of nearby classical monuments – some of which were conveniently circular in shape. From now on, the building was to be entered in standard Christian fashion from the west. They did not, however, use the large existing west door of the pagan temple, but made a small entrance to the right of it. Or so, at least, archaeologists have ingeniously concluded – pointing not only to the pattern of wear on the floor but also to the fact that more early Christian graffiti are found on the columns leading up to this side door than anywhere else on the building (graffiti being a sure sign of human traffic). This reversal of the orientation was to cause endless confusion among the first antiquarians to visit the site, Pausanias in hand. They did not realise that their ancient guide had entered the temple from the east, rather than – as they did – the west; and so they were condemned to matching up his description to what remained of the building 'back to front'.

Inside, there was even less work for the Christian builders to do. They did not have to face the awkward task of clearing away Pheidias' vast showpiece statue of Athena. That must have been long destroyed – if not before, then in a terrible fire which struck the Parthenon in the third century AD. There was almost certainly a less grand replacement, or a whole series of them – the last of which would have fallen victim to the new religion. A charmingly unreliable anecdote told in the biography of Proclus, a fifth-century neo-Platonist, has the goddess deciding to move in with the philosopher when her statue was 'taken away by those people who move things which should not be moved' (that is, the Christians). Eviction had not lessened Athena's capacity to command: appearing to Proclus in a dream, she ordered him to be quick about making his house ready. Where once she had stood in the temple, they made the nave of the new church, complete with pulpit, screen and bishop's throne. This throne was, in fact, a splendid remnant from the classical past, a marble chair (which still survives) covered in sculpture and featuring a dramatic winged figure that might just have passed for a rather menacing breed of angel. Three new doors gave access to what had been the back room of the temple, but which now became the church foyer (or narthex), with a baptistery and font in one corner. To bring in more light, a row of windows was added high up on each side, cutting in several places right through the sculpted frieze, while the outer colonnade was effectively turned into a screening wall by infilling the spaces between the columns to roughly half their height.

All that remained was to do something about the pagan sculpture. At the sacred east end, the scene of the birth of Athena would hardly have suited the new church and was promptly removed from the pediment. The old metope panels presented a trickier problem. It would have required major demolition to take them down, so along most of three sides of the building they were systematically defaced, hacked away until their subjects were unrecognisable. It is not entirely clear why the rest of the sculpture escaped this treatment. The frieze was probably not visible enough to

5. The early Christians saw the Annunciation in the scene on this metope –
and so spared it from their chisel. In fact, it was almost certainly the
goddesses Athena (on the right) and Hera (left) masquerading as the Virgin
Mary and the angel Gabriel.

trouble them, and in any case depicted a relatively anodyne (or, at least, not demonstratively pagan) procession. One metope, at the north-west corner, is generally thought to have avoided the Christian chisel because its bona fide classical scene looked for all the world like the Annunciation (*Illustration 5*). Maybe the west pediment escaped for similar reasons, its contest between Athena and Poseidon given a suitably biblical interpretation. Christians are known to have been commendably inventive in dreaming up such iconographic parallels. One priceless Roman cameo, for example, showing the emperor lording it over a heap of vanquished barbarians was for centuries identified as Joseph at the court of the Egyptian pharaoh. So who knows what might have been perceived in these two rival deities? But most mysterious of all is the survival of the metopes which ran along the south side of the building. Why deface all the other panels, barring the single 'Annunciation', and not bother with these? It is hard to read any obvious Christian message in the mythical Battle of Greeks and Centaurs that forms the major theme here – a band of plucky fighters locked in combat with monstrous, drunken crossbreeds, half-human, half-horse. Yet it is equally hard to believe that the south side avoided the Christians' sanitising treatment simply because it was not visible from the main thoroughfare across the Acropolis. Whatever the reasoning, the fact that any group of metopes survives from the Parthenon at all (including some of the most dramatic marble sculpture to have decorated the building (*Illustration 18*)) is down to the choices and decisions of some Christian Athenians of the sixth century AD, whose motives are almost entirely lost to us.

When, more than half a millennium later, Michael

6. The Christian church of Our Lady of Athens neatly adapted and reorientated the classical temple. What had been the main eastern entrance of the Parthenon is now the Christian sanctuary with it distinctive apse (shown here after its twelfth-century enlargement). The sculpted frieze survives, except for the central slab; the outer colonnade of the temple acts as a screening wall around the church.

Choniates came to take his seat on the marble bishop's throne in the cathedral of Our Lady of Athens, the building had recently been given an even grander makeover (*Illustration 6*). It was most likely under his immediate predecessor that the small apse at the east end was demolished to make way for a much more substantial version, extending out so far that it now abutted the ancient columns and required the complete removal of the central slab of the frieze. This slab (it depicts the famous '*peplos* scene'; see below, Chapter 5) is now in the British Museum and was found by Elgin's workmen built into the Acropolis fortifications. Michael himself may have sponsored a lavish new scheme of interior decoration in the church, featuring a painting of the Last Judgement on the wall of the entrance porch, scenes from the Passion in the narthex, as well as a whole gallery of saints and bishops. Almost nothing of this is now visible, beyond a few decidedly uninspiring daubs of colour. But much more survived up to the 1880s, albeit – as the then Marquess of Bute complained – 'in a lamentable state of decay'. Lamentable or not, there was certainly enough still preserved for him to commission a series of watercolours documenting the Christian paintings in the Parthenon, and it is mainly from these that we can deduce the subject matter and hazard a reasonable guess at a date, somewhere in the late twelfth century. At around the same time, a mosaic was installed in the ceiling of the apse. This has long since fallen to pieces, but in the Parthenon collection in the British Museum is a group of 188 tesserae, mostly glass, some gilded, some in red or emerald-green stone, 'from the Ceiling of the Parthenon', as their original label said, 'when a Greek Church'. They were discovered in the 1830s when debris around the apse was cleared, and acquired in 1848 from a Briton resident in Athens. Well into the nineteenth century it was a favourite Sunday afternoon occupation for the schoolchildren of the city to go up to the Acropolis to hunt for tesserae. The gold ones must have been the most prized.

Twelfth-century Athens may have been down-at-heel, but it certainly had, or could attract, enough money to make something very special of its cathedral. No wonder Michael admired it so keenly, as did others, before and after him. In 1018 the Byzantine emperor Basil II ('the Bulgar Slayer', as he was later called) had come to the city especially to visit Our Lady of Athens. Basil is now best known for his victory over the Bulgarian empire (hence his title) and, in popular legend at least, for a notorious atrocity: he is said to have blinded almost 15,000 of the opposing army, sparing the sight of just one man in a hundred so that they could lead the others home. True or not, he showed a less thuggish side at Athens, where he turned some of his booty into gifts for the cathedral – including, it would seem, that famous golden dove.

More than two centuries later, the cathedral was one of the sacred sites described by an Italian traveller, Niccolò da Martoni, in his *Pilgrimage Book*, which survives as a manuscript in the Bibliothèque Nationale in Paris. Niccolò passed through Athens on 24 and 25 February 1395 and the account of his visit (written in rather lumpish Latin) includes the first systematic description of the Parthenon and its contents to survive since Pausanias. It is a striking combination of gushing enthusiasm for the architecture and decoration with a pilgrim's focus on holy relics and, in the words of one recent writer, 'Christian bric-à-brac'. Niccolò is amazed at the size of it all, at the marble carving, and the sheer number of columns (he managed to get to 60; in fact there were 58). 'It seems impossible for the mind of man to conceive', he muses, 'how such a vast building could have been constructed.' Inside, he picks out the magnificent *ciborium*, or baldachino, around the altar – a canopy supported on four columns of jasper. And he tells a magnificent yarn about the cathedral doors, which had once, he claims, been the gates of the famous city of Troy, brought to Athens when it finally fell to the Greeks. Who had spun him this preposterous story, we do not know – church cleaner, cleric or pilgrim guide. But at least it served to keep alive the links between the medieval monument and the traditions of the classical past.

For Niccolò, however, the cathedral's renown comes no less from its specifically Christian history and associations. This is not just the predictable selection of anatomical relics, though it can certainly boast some cherished bones, skulls and fingers from a respectable group of saints. Nor is it only a question of that other medieval favourite, an icon of the Virgin Mary, painted by the very hand of Saint Luke himself, though there is a beautiful example of just that, inlaid with pearls and precious stones and kept under lock and key in a chapel near the altar. A more unusual treasure, and, according to Niccolò, a particularly prized possession of the cathedral, is a copy of the gospels, transcribed in Greek on gilded vellum by St Helena, the pious mother of Constantine, the first Roman emperor officially to convert to Christianity. And one revered graffito took the Christian message right back into the history of the pagan temple. Pilgrims like Niccolò were obviously shown the sign of the cross said to have been scratched onto one of the cathedral columns by Saint Dionysius the Areopagite. This Dionysius has a walk-on part in the Acts of the Apostles, where he is converted by Saint Paul on his visit to Athens (hence 'Areopagite', after the Areopagus Hill where Paul preached), and he is now most widely known for lending his name to the main road that runs round the south of the Acropolis in the modern city. But a Christian tradition grew up, fanciful as it almost certainly was, that Dionysius had been at the Parthenon on the day when Jesus was crucified and had witnessed from its colonnade the earthquake that marked the occasion. Understanding something of its significance ('either the structure of the cosmos is about to collapse or the Son of God to undergo something terrible'), he inscribed a cross on the column by which he was standing. It is a neat story that both recognises the pagan past of the building and conscripts it into a Christian narrative.

THE RENAISSANCE PARTHENON

By the time of Niccolò's visit, the Byzantine empire had lost its hold on Athens. Although the Fourth Crusade had originally set its sights on Jerusalem, it soon found that Byzantine territories offered easier pickings. Michael Choniates made a shrewd assessment of the military strength that confronted the town and surrendered Athens to the Crusaders in 1204 before they had a chance to sack it. The worst casualty seems to have been the archbishop's carefully assembled library, ransacked and plundered from the cupboards in the cathedral where it had been stored. Michael himself beat a sensible retreat and spent the rest of his life on an island near by, looking across the water at Athens (and, over 16 years, daring only one brief visit to his old home). Meanwhile a rich

Burgundian warlord, Othon de la Roche, took control and a French archbishop was installed in the cathedral. The Parthenon's official title became, for a short while at least, 'Notre Dame d'Athènes'.

Over the next 250 years or so, a series of mercenary invasions, military coups and diplomatic trade-offs passed control of Athens from the Franks to the Catalans and, finally, to a well-known family of Florentine bankers, the Acciaiuoli, with the Venetian and Ottoman Turks constantly hovering in the background. For most of their rule, in fact, the Acciaiuoli paid protection money, more politely known as 'tribute', to the Turkish sultan – until 1456, when Mehmed II, 'the Conqueror', took advantage of their family quarrels and annexed the duchy (though some of the Acciaiuoli held out on the Acropolis for two more years). Throughout this period, Athens witnessed a strange cultural mix, as various western traditions of chivalry, troubadours, tournaments and courtly love made different accommodations with the town's classical past and its contemporary Greek inhabitants. King Pedro IV of Aragon, for example, one of the powers behind the Catalan mercenaries who lorded it over Athens in the early fourteenth century, enthused about the ancient Parthenon, calling it 'the most precious jewel that exists in the world, and such that all the Kings of Christendom could in vain imitate'; his wife, on the other hand, was more interested in getting her hands on some of the precious Christian relics lodged in the cathedral. The Acciaiuoli too straddled different cultures. Under their rule, starting in 1387, Greek was reintroduced as the official language (after almost two centuries of French and Spanish), and they protected the Greek Orthodox church. But on the Acropolis itself, they converted the ancient gateway, or Propylaia (once, we assume, the residence of Michael Choniates and other arch-bishops), into a magnificent Renaissance fortified palazzo. It would have looked perfectly at home in quattrocento Florence.

None of this affected the cathedral very much. Its title kept pace with the changing nationalities in control of the town (Seu de Santa Maria de Cetinas, Sta Maria di Atene); archbishops, from different countries and from different wings of the Christian faith came and went; its furniture and internal layout presumably adjusted to the shifts between Latin and Orthodox liturgy. It celebrated a number of royal weddings and funerals, and on one occasion (20 May 1380, to be precise) it hosted a special meeting of the Catalan junta at which they drafted a plea for military protection to Pedro IV. But there was very little structural change. The Acciaiuoli proved to be lavish benefactors. The will of the first of them, Nerio, provided for inlaying the cathedral doors with silver, and he even bequeathed the town itself to the church. It was as if, henceforth, the Parthenon was to own Athens, though the practical significance of this gesture is far from clear.

The most lasting addition of this whole period, probably built soon after the arrival of the Crusaders, was a tower in the right-hand corner of the entrance porch; it was partly constructed, as archaeologists have recently deduced, from blocks cannibalised from the back of the tomb of a Roman grandee, the so-called Monument of Philopappus (whose façade – or what is left of it – still dominates the skyline of the Hill of the Muses, half a kilometre or so from the Acropolis). Its original purpose was probably to act as a bell-tower for the cathedral, but it also had the effect of blocking off the small door that had for centuries provided the main access to the narthex; the central west doorway of the old Parthenon must at this point have come back into regular use, soon to be embellished by Nerio's bequest of silver. The tower, with its internal spiral staircase, still survives up to the roofline. It has proved remarkably adaptable: the Turks made it into a minaret in their new Parthenon mosque and through the nineteenth and twentieth centuries it offered generations of antiquarians and archaeologists convenient access to the sculptures of the frieze and pediment still in place at the temple's west end.

It was during the rule of the Acciaiuoli that the first sur- viving drawing of the Parthenon was produced, the work of the Italian businessman-cum-papal diplomat whose glowing description of the 'marvellous temple of Pallas Athena' we noted in Chapter 1. Cyriaco de' Pizzicolli – or Cyriac of Ancona, as he is now commonly known – visited Athens twice, in 1436 and 1444. He may well have lodged on the Acropolis itself and, on the second occasion certainly, he went to pay his respects to the Acciaiuoli in their splendid palazzo in the Propylaia. On both visits he made reams of detailed notes and drawings. Many of these were destroyed in 1514, in a terrible fire in the library in Pesaro where they were kept, but reworkings and copies of various sections, a few made by Cyriac himself, the rest by quite other hands, have survived. The drawing of the Parthenon shown in *Illustration 7* is more likely than most to be Cyriac's own. It is accurate in several crucial essentials: eight columns in the right (Doric) order; the position of the metope panels (*epis- tilia*) appropriately marked; the presence of the frieze (*listae parietum*) correctly noted, with a section drawn out. The

[65]

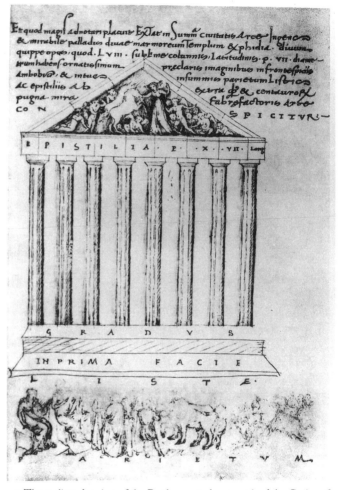

7. The earliest drawing of the Parthenon to have survived, by Cyriac of Ancona (or a close copy of his work), who visited in the mid-fifteenth century. The notes in Latin above the drawing give a brief description of the temple and call it 'a divine work by Pheidias'.

building has, however, become strangely elongated; and the sculptures in the pediment hardly show a convincing struggle between Athena and Poseidon, but something more like a fifteenth-century lady (Athena?) dealing with a pair of troublesome horses, backed up by a chorus of little Renaissance *putti*.

All the same, Cyriac has become a founding hero of modern archaeological studies and is credited as 'the first traveller since antiquity to describe the Parthenon' (which is, of course, to draw a discreet veil over Niccolò da Martoni). In modern scholarly terms he does seem to have a lot to recommend him. He gets the vital statistics broadly correct (he adds up the number of columns to an exact 58, as against Niccolò's 60); he rightly deduces that the best-preserved metope panels show the battles of Greeks and Centaurs; and he provides the first ever surviving written reference to the sculpted frieze (which, he guesses, 'represented the victories of Athens in the time of Pericles'). But his fame is no less dependent on what he decides to leave out of his description. For he makes no mention whatsoever of the cathedral of the Virgin; unlike Niccolò, Cyriac sees straight through the Christian layout and lavish medieval decoration to the fabric of the ancient temple lying just below the surface. For all the strange proportions and the unsettling Renaissance tinge given to the sculpture in the pediment, his drawing has been hailed as a brilliant archaeological attempt to unthink the later 'accretions' so as to reveal the classical structure beneath.

And so it is. It is at the same time, of course, a wilful refusal to acknowledge the appearance of the building in his own day or to see more in it than a relic of classical antiquity. In fact, by the time the new Turkish rulers converted the

Parthenon into a mosque in the early 1460s, it had been a Christian church for just about as long as it had ever been a pagan temple. But most modern scholars (and tourist guides) have followed Cyriac in turning a blind eye to the glories of the Parthenon in its guise of Our Lady of Athens.

'PLATO'S ACADEMY'

An even blinder eye has been turned to the mosque that was the next metamorphosis of the Parthenon. The plain fact is that less attention has been devoted to the monuments of Turkish Greece than to any other period of the country's archaeology. It is one legacy of that curious combination of civil war, amateur freedom-fighting and professional atrocity (on both sides), now heroically cast as the Greek War of Independence, that Turkish rule has been almost universally painted as destructive and oppressive; a very nasty blot on the Greek landscape and, for the most part, better ignored if not decried. Vested interests are still so strong that even now it is impossible to reach any reasonable judgement on the merits and failings of the *turkokratia* (as the period of Turkish rule is called in Greek). It would be hopelessly naïve just to turn the usual prejudice on its head and suggest that the Ottoman rulers were all enlightened and benevolent. They were not. But, over its 375 years, their rule was certainly more varied than is generally assumed, and not always so very different from what had gone before, under Florentines, Catalans, Franks – or, for that matter, under the Byzantine administration (which, in Michael Choniates' day at least, had squeezed the Greeks hard). So far as the Parthenon itself is concerned, it has been easy to paint the Turks as the agents of its destruction (they after all put their powder there, even if the Venetians fired the cannonballs). But, as we shall see, the building's life as a Turkish mosque is notable for its continuity with its Christian and pagan past.

Mehmed II, Athens' first sultan, was a classic blend of cultivated connoisseur and ruthless conqueror. By the end of his reign in 1481 he had taken Constantinople (and turned it into his new capital), driven Ottoman rule into Greece and the Balkans and set his sights on Rhodes and southern Italy; he had also poured vast amounts of money into science and the arts, sponsored universities, assembled libraries and commissioned work from top-flight Italian artists (his son reputedly asked Michelangelo to design a Bosphorus bridge – but pressure of work on the Sistine Chapel put paid to the idea). As soon as the Acciaiuoli had finally surrendered in 1458, the new ruler paid a four-day royal visit to Athens. According to his Greek biography (another of the sultan's commissions – and not noted for its critical tone), Mehmed was 'absolutely passionate' about the town and its famous sights, having already heard tell of all the amazing achievements of the ancient Athenians. Unlike Michael, he was not disappointed, and it was the Acropolis in particular that impressed him – as he managed 'to work out from the surviving remains how it had been long ago'. Indeed, as his biographer crows, out of respect for their ancestors he gave the Athenians everything they wanted.

Not quite everything, presumably. For the Acropolis was in fact turned into the Turkish garrison base. The disdar or garrison commander, took up residence in the Florentines' palazzo. And, with a wry sense of humour (or as a gross insult to local sensibilities, depending on how you see it), the Turks converted the small temple known as the Erechtheion, which had also had a long history as a church, into a harem: the famous porch with its line-up of caryatids now doing duty as an advertisement for the delights that lay inside. Before long the whole hill seems to have been effectively closed to outsiders, and travellers' tales in the Turkish period feature anecdotes about whom you had to bribe, and how much, to gain access to the Acropolis. In 1675 Dr Jacob Spon of Lyon and his English friend, George Wheler Esq., resorted to coffee to persuade a reluctant disdar, or 'Governour', to grant them entry: 'an old Souldier of the Castle', Wheler wrote, 'his Friend and Confident, for three *Oka's* of *Coffee*, two to the Governour, and one to himself, perswaded him at last to give way'. The church in the Parthenon was meanwhile converted into what Wheler was to call 'the finest Mosque in the world': all it required was a minaret (easily adapted from the bell-tower), the removal of some of the Christian furniture (what happened to the holy relics is anyone's guess) and a quick coat of whitewash over the most obvious Christian decoration.

A combination of factors took Athens and the Acropolis off the map of most western travellers for many years at the beginning of Turkish rule: it was not only a question of the obstacles imposed by the Turkish garrison on any exploration of Athenian antiquities; equally off-putting were the periodic bouts of war between the Venetians and Turks through the sixteenth and seventeenth centuries, which made travel to the eastern Mediterranean even less safe than it had been before. Some visitors who did make it to Athens almost certainly failed in their attempts to get up to the Acropolis. One French traveller, for example, writing in 1632, notes that the

Parthenon was now a mosque and records the local myth that it had actually been the 'Temple of the Unknown God' in which St Paul had preached; he also assures his readers that the building 'is oval in shape'. We can only imagine that he saw it from a considerable distance away. Others, who did not venture a visit, seem to have despaired of Athens entirely. In 1575 a professor at the University of Tübingen wrote to some of his friends in Greece to inquire whether the town had been entirely destroyed. Replies assured him that it had not. One even referred to the Parthenon, though in a strangely off-key way: the letter talked of the Athenian 'Pantheon' (like the famous monument in Rome) and attributed its sculpture not to Pheidias, but to the fourth-century artist Praxiteles.

By far the most interesting description of the Parthenon in this period (arguably in any period) comes from the hand of a Turkish traveller, Evliya Celebi; western Europeans were not, we should remember, the only tourists in the world. Evliya was born in 1611, the son of the sultan's chief jeweller, and – thanks to an ample legacy and some convenient diplomatic assignments – managed to devote his whole life to travel throughout and beyond the Ottoman empire, from Syria to Denmark. The account of this extraordinary *Wanderlust* made up a *Book of Travels* that was published in 10 volumes. Despite its obvious charisma, Evliya's work is not well known, or highly rated, in the West. Its Arabic Turkish is far out of the reach of the vast majority of us and has been translated into most European languages only in selections (sadly Sir Elmer Bole, the student and translator of Evliya in A. S. Byatt's *The Biographer's Tale*, is pure fiction). Besides, its curious and often flagrantly unbelievable anecdotes, combined with a good number of outright errors, have not endeared the *Book of Travels* to those who value accuracy beyond all else.

Evliya's description of Athens, which he visited more than once in the 1630s and 40s, has suffered on both counts. It has never been fully translated into English and it includes some truly wondrous myths (or atrocious howlers). At one point, for example, Evliya claims that Athens was founded by Solomon – a reflection, at best, of some inventive local tradition attempting to tie the town into the grand sweep of biblical history, but more likely an implausible fantasy; unless perhaps, as some commentators have tried to rationalise it, in talking to his local informants Evliya misheard 'Solomon' for 'Solon', the great Athenian law-giver and founding father. But, mistakes and all, Evliya offers a vivid and often carefully observed account of the mosque on the Acropolis. Instead of our usual view of the Turks as the Acropolis's burly gatekeepers (the only question being whether you could bribe them or not), we have for once a Turkish view of the building; and one that gives us a glimpse of the Parthenon's popular fame and heady mythology in the mid-seventeeth century.

Evliya makes it very clear indeed that the conversion into a mosque had had little effect on the inside of the building. The baldachino over the altar that had so struck Niccolò still held pride of place, even though the altar itself had been removed. Its four columns of red marble shone so brightly that you could see the colour of your face reflected in them; they were just like 'the philosopher's stone' and each one, Evliya guesses, was worth a whole country's tax revenue – a characteristically Ottoman calculation. To judge from this and other accounts, Niccolò had been wrong to call the material of these columns jasper. He had presumably mis-remembered, or mixed up his notes, for there were, according to Evliya, four columns 'of emerald green … carved with amazing flowers' near the 'minber' (pulpit), which in the cathedral had formed the division between the sanctuary and the body of the church; and pieces of both green and red marble have, in fact, been found in the debris on site. But even the plain white marble was something special. The marble floor was made of slabs 10 feet square, and brilliantly polished; each of the blocks in the walls were 'as big as an elephant' and so expertly fitted together that you could not detect the joins ('you would think the wall was made from a single block'); and there were wall panels at the east end so sheer that they let the sunlight shine through. Other writers too were overcome by this miraculous translucence; and Messrs Spon and Wheler offered a learned classical explanation, suggesting that the stone was none other than 'Phengytes', a transparent marble mentioned in Pliny's great encyclopaedia as a favourite of the emperor Nero.

Of course, not everything survived from the Parthenon's days as a cathedral. 'In the time of the infidel' (that is the Christians), Evliya explains, the great doors had been decorated 'with solid gold and diamonds'; but all this had been removed, although its settings were still clearly visible. Evliya is probably on the right lines here, even if wrong in detail: it was presumably Nerio Acciaiuoli's silver inlay that had been taken off by the Turks. But as for the ancient sculpture and Christian paintings, the coating of whitewash that various writers refer to must have been selectively, or at least thinly, applied. For Evliya could see them well enough to give a remarkably upbeat description. The sculptures he attributes to an artist called Aristos (as this is Greek for 'excellent', the most likely guess is that somewhere along the line 'an excellent craftsman' had turned into a proper name), and he sees their subject 'as all the creatures fashioned by the Creator of the Universe, from Adam to the Second Coming'. He devotes most of his attention, though, to an elaborate painting of the Last Judgement whose faint traces archaeologists have detected in the cathedral porch, 'drinking and dancing in the gardens of Paradise' on the one side, 'fire and demons' on the other. In a suitably breathless paragraph he lists an extraordinary range of figures, pagan, Christian and Moslem intermingled: 'demons, satans and wild beasts and devils and enchantresses and angels and dragons and antichrists and one eyed monsters and those with a hundred shapes and crocodiles and elephants and rhinoceroses ... and what is more Cherubim, Gabriel, Seraphim, Asra-el, Michael, the ninth heaven with the throne of God, the bridge of a hair's breadth, the scales of judgement ...', and so on. It is all so moving, he says, that when anyone looks at these paintings of hell, 'they are taken aback, overcome with fear, struck dumb and lose their breath'.

One puzzle is that Evliya has nothing to say of the mosaic whose gold and coloured glass tesserae once scattered the site. But other writers of the period, Spon and Wheler included, were not so reticent. They talk of an image of (predictably enough) the Holy Virgin, covering the apse behind what had been the altar. And they tell the old chestnut of a story about a Turk who once upon a time took a potshot at it, only to find soon after that his hand withered away. From that moment on, they claim, the Turks decided to inflict no further damage on the image. Be that as it may, the impression we get from all the writers of the Ottoman period is that the Turks were not the uncompromising iconoclasts they are often assumed to be. They may perhaps have continued the defacement of the metope panels (destruction of this sort is always hard to date). But, by and large, they did considerably less harm to the fabric of the building or its existing decoration than the Christians had in converting the pagan temple into a cathedral a millennium earlier. For most of its history as a mosque, barring the occasional splash of whitewash, Moslem worship took place in the Parthenon under the watchful eye of the Christian paintings and the mosaic of the Virgin Mary.

But just as important as his description of the present state of the mosque are Evliya's often far-fetched anecdotes about its history. These were presumably picked up from the local residents on one of his visits, perhaps even on a guided tour round the sights of the Acropolis. As such, they take us directly back to the popular traditions that clustered around the Parthenon in the mid-seventeenth century, and to the kind of stories that locals, whether Greek or Turk, would tell to a high-ranking and curious Turkish tourist. At one point, for example, Evliya stops to notice a huge basin in the mosque's porch – a feature remarked on by other travellers (and, in fact, parts of it still survive). It gives Evliya a rare opportunity for some moralising. It was big enough 'to hold five men at the same time, and in those far-off days the temple's founder filled it up for his workmen to drink' – not with water, but 'shameless wine'. It is easy enough to imagine a seventeenth-century guide making this a highlight of a Parthenon tour. But most striking of all is the starring role that Evliya gives to the 'divine' philosopher Plato (Ephlatoun in Turkish). For not only was Plato supposed to be responsible for those miraculous translucent panels in the east wall, but it was from the splendid marble throne in the apse that he used to 'teach and advise the people'. In Evliya's account – and no doubt much more widely in the common talk of his time – the Parthenon had become mythologised as 'Plato's Academy'.

THE BIG BANG

The luckiest chapter in the whole history of modern studies of the Parthenon came in 1674, three decades or so after Evliya's visit. From the 1660s on (aided in due course by a temporary lull in hostilities between Turks and Venetians) Athens became a more popular destination for visitors from the west. In fact the whole genre of travellers' tales, recounting the adventures of their journey to Greece, combined with learned (or sometimes less learned) disquisitions on the classical remains, became so popular that it generated its own forgeries. One of the best-selling accounts of such a visit, by a certain André-Georges Guillet de la Guilletière, was eventually unmasked as the armchair work of a man who had never set foot in Greece (though, significantly perhaps, his book included almost as many correct observations and interpretations of the remains as it did blunders). At the same time, maverick enthusiasts for dangerous travel in far-flung classical lands were increasingly joined by the mainstream of the European aristocracy. One such aristocrat was the French ambassador to the Ottoman court, the Marquis de Nointel, who visited Athens in 1674 with a princely retinue, including the obligatory artist. This artist, often referred to as Jacques Carrey (though his identity is quite uncertain), produced for his patron a set of drawings of more than half the surviving ancient sculpture of the Parthenon (*Illustration 8*). These are no less an aesthetic product of their time than the Renaissance version of Cyriac of Ancona. But they match modern standards of archaeological accuracy much more closely, and – if, as is almost certain, they were drawn from the ground without the aid of scaffolding – are an absolute triumph of observation. If it were not for these, we would have very little idea of the character of much of the original sculpture (including most of the west pediment). It was a lucky chapter indeed, because, just 13 years later, on 28 September 1687, a huge amount was utterly lost in a vast explosion and its aftermath.

The Turks had, on the most generous interpretation, very bad luck with their gunpowder stores. In 1645, the stores in the Propylaia were struck by lightning, killing the disdar's family as well as seriously damaging the building. When Athens was again under attack in 1687, this time from Venetian forces of a Holy League formed against the Ottoman empire, they chose to put their ammunition (together with their women and children) in the Parthenon instead. Perhaps, as one Venetian historian suggested, they trusted the 'thickness of the walls and arches'; or maybe they thought the opposing Christian forces would not seek to destroy a building that had been for so long a famous church. Either way, they were badly mistaken. The Venetian army was under the local control of a Swedish general, Count Koenigsmark, who bombarded the building. Surviving marks on the west front alone show where around 700 cannonballs hit their target, and several of the murderous

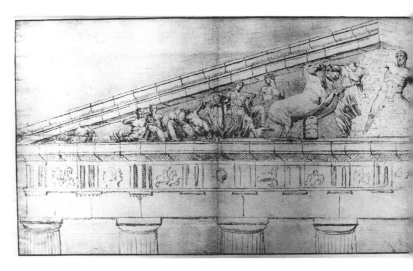

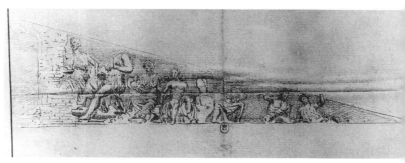

8. These seventeenth-century drawings of the west pediment have offered the crucial key to its original arrangement. The central group shows Athena in contest with the god Poseidon for control of Athens and its territory. Behind the battling deities come their chariot teams (Poseidon's horses had already disappeared by the date of the drawing); and in the angles other gods, goddesses and local legendary heroes assist or look on. The happy couple on the extreme left are the pair that many early travellers (wrongly) identified as the Roman emperor Hadrian and his wife Sabina (p. 140).

VEDUTA DEL CAST: D'ACROPOLIS DALLA PARTE DI TRAMONTA

9. A Venetian view of the explosion of 1687. The gunpowder sends the roof of the mosque flying into the air, though the minaret appears so far unharmed. Around the Parthenon the houses of the garrison village are just visible above the fortifications. On the right a flag waves from the top of the Frankish Tower, which had been built by the Acciaiuoli before the Turkish conquest and remained a well-known landmark until its controversial demolition in 1875 (pp. 108–9).

missiles themselves have been discovered on the site. In the end, the inevitable happened and the ammunition store ignited in a vast explosion, killing as many as 300 people (usually forgotten in the story of archaeological tragedy) and blowing out the centre of the building, smashing 28 columns, parts of the frieze and the internal rooms that had served for church and mosque (*Illustration 9*). The west pediment survived the bombardment itself more or less intact, but when General Morosini, the overall Venetian commander, arrived on the scene to enjoy the victory, he decided he would take the central figures back to Venice. They did not make it. The machinery he was using to lower them from their setting broke and they crashed to the ground. Only a few fragments were taken off to Italy by Morosini's opportunistic subordinates (one of which, a rather battered head, is now in the Louvre). The other sorry remains were left on site to be found by Lord Elgin's agents and later archaeologists. From this point on, the history of the Parthenon is the history of a ruin.

For once, we have an eye-witness account from a woman. Several letters from Anna Åkerhjelm, a lady-in-waiting to Countess Koenigsmark, have survived, describing to her brother the events as she saw them. 'How it dismayed His Excellency,' she wrote, 'to destroy the beautiful temple that has existed three thousand years and is called the Temple of Minerva! In vain however: the bombs did their work so effectively that never in this world can the temple be replaced.' Åkerhjelm did, however, find a memento of the building and its destruction. When she was wandering round the site of the Parthenon shortly after the final Turkish sur-render, she picked up a precious Arabic manuscript that had somehow survived the explosion in the mosque. It was later given by Åkerhjelm's brother to the library of Uppsala ('a rare manuscript from Greece', as the letter of thanks from the librarian describes it), one of the most unexpected fragments of the diaspora of the Parthenon, and its contents, across western Europe.

4

FROM RUIN TO RECONSTRUCTION

The explosion of 1687 put the Parthenon, once and for all, out of practical use after more than two millennia as temple, church and mosque. It created a much more dilapidated ruin than the one we know today. 'Our' Parthenon, with its instantly recognisable silhouette, is a recreation of the early twentieth century. What the explosion left behind was a scatter of debris and a cluster of columns at each end. As J. P. Mahaffy put it, with characteristic frankness, some decades before the major restoration programme: the damage was such that 'from the city below, the front and rear of the temple look like the remains of two different buildings'.

In political terms, the consequences of the explosion and of the victory of the Holy League were minimal. Within a few months the Venetians decided not to hold on to Athens: they hardly had the military resources to defend it successfully, and in any case an outbreak of plague made the town a decidedly unattractive proposition. The Turks returned to the Acropolis, rebuilding their garrison village on a smaller scale. At some point soon after (we do not know exactly when), they put up a small mosque in the middle of the Parthenon's ruins. This building was still standing in 1839, when it was captured on the first surviving photograph of the

10. The earliest known photograph of the Parthenon, taken in 1839. In the centre of the ruin the small Turkish mosque still stands (serving as a makeshift museum). Note that now just two figures remain, just visible, in the west pediment, the so-called 'Hadrian and Sabina' (p. 140).

Acropolis (*Illustration 10*). By then it had come to serve as a museum for the first discoveries made on the site after the War of Independence. It was not demolished until 1844.

For the Parthenon itself, however, the consequences were devastating. As soon as it became a ruin, it lost the protection that its status as working church or mosque had provided; and, like most ruins, it became increasingly ruinous. In effect, for more than 100 years there was an open season on the Parthenon's fabric and remaining sculpture. Locals found it a convenient supply of building stone, they ground its marble down for lime and they broke whole blocks apart to find the lead clamps within. Visitors from abroad had plenty of horror stories to tell. 'It is to be regretted that so much admirable sculpture as is still extant about this fabric should be all likely to perish … from ignorant contempt and brutal violence', lamented Richard Chandler of Magdalen College Oxford, who visited in the 1770s, courtesy of the Society of Dilettanti. 'Numerous carved stones have disappeared; and many, lying in the ruinous heaps, moved our indignation at the barbarism daily exercised in defacing them.' And, 30 years later, Edward Dodwell had yet more specific charges to level. 'Large masses of Pentelic marble were broken into smaller pieces for the construction of the miserable cottages of the garrison,' he wrote, 'while others, and particularly the bas-reliefs, were burnt into lime; for the Turks *are said* to have preferred for that purpose a sculptured block to a plain one, though the material was the same. Such is the pleasure with which uncivilised ignorance or frantic superstition, destroyed in a moment the works of years, and the admiration of ages.'

Archaeology suggests that the substance of these allegations is broadly true. But, true or not, stories of local barbarism and neglect provided useful cover for the activities of many of the foreign visitors themselves. For very few travellers reached the Acropolis without casting a predatory eye on the sculpture lying about or built into the 'miserable cottages'. Some of these were grand-scale collectors, such as the Comte de Choiseul-Gouffier, the French equivalent of Lord Elgin, ambassador to the sultan's court and a single-minded connoisseur. In the 1780s, through the good Turkish connections of his agent and a combination of persistence and bribery, he got hold of his metope and frieze-slab, now in the Louvre. The agent even managed to acquire a second metope (which had reputedly fallen from the temple during a storm), but this was stowed on a ship captured by Lord Nelson and was later bought by Elgin. Others were relatively modest souvenir hunters, content with an elegant head or foot fallen from, or (more realistically) chiselled off, the frieze or metopes. Chandler himself is probably typical when, after his tirade against the ignorance of the residents, he writes, 'We purchased two fine fragments of the freeze [sic], which we found inserted over door-ways in the town; and were presented with a beautiful trunk, which had fallen from the metopes, and lay neglected in the garden of a Turk.' It was in the pockets of such gentlemen that many of the smaller pieces, now scattered through the museums of Europe, originally left the Acropolis. As Chandler hints, the locals must soon have turned their energies to just this kind of traffic. It was much more lucrative, after all, to flog a fragment of Pheidias to a visiting milord than to grind it into mortar.

Some of these souvenirs have, predictably enough, gone astray. No one knows what has happened to Chandler's three prized acquisitions. Others have had notably perilous histories. One of the pieces of frieze now in the British Museum, for example, did not come via Lord Elgin at all, but was dug up in 1902, in a garden rockery at an Essex mansion, Colne Park; it was unearthed along with a Greek inscription last seen in 1771 when it had been the property of a 'Mr Jones'. The best guess is that these were both part of a small consignment of antiquities assembled by James Stuart, who was in Athens in the 1750s with his partner Nicholas Revett, drawing and surveying the Parthenon for the Society of Dilettanti (work eventually published as Volume II of their hugely influential *Antiquities of Athens* in 1789 – though tactfully dated 1787, the year before Stuart's death). Stuart is known to have sent some cargo on to Smyrna, where he planned to meet it, but it 'miscarried'. 'Mr Jones' was later given the inscription, and presumably the sculpture too, by a naval captain. At this point the trail goes cold. But the likelihood is that both pieces somehow found their way together into the collection of Thomas Astle, a renowned antiquarian, manuscript collector and trustee of the British Museum, whose son was to own Colne Park. What furious bout of spring-cleaning, distaste for family heirlooms or 'uncivilised ignorance' then consigned a notable fragment of the Parthenon frieze into the bedding of an English rock garden, we have simply no idea.

ELGIN'S MARBLES

This is the context in which we must see the events of 1801 to 1811, when Lord Elgin or his agents (most of the time Elgin was not himself present) were busy, on and off, collecting antiquities in Athens and elsewhere in Greece, and dispatching them, by the boatload to England. At the very top of their wish-list was the Parthenon. Roughly half its surviving sculpture was removed: some of it was picked up from where it had fallen, some excavated near by, some, notoriously, was taken down from its original position on the building itself. Our own modern image of a clean, sanitised Acropolis, with the Parthenon as its centrepiece, a substantial free standing monument, unencumbered by later structures and fiercely protected from interference, makes Elgin's actions almost unimaginable. (For how could anyone but a villain have laid a chisel on such a monument …?) But it was not 'our' Parthenon that was at issue. Elgin's building was a much more ruined affair: it was colonised by a mosque, encroached by a garrison shanty-town and for more than a century had been despoiled by locals and visitors alike; and it was under the control of a now time-expired Ottoman government whose corruption was mixed with, and no doubt mitigated by, inefficiency. The one clear fact about Elgin's interventions is that he did not ransack an 'archaeological site' in any sense that we would recognise. He removed, more systematically – indeed more ruthlessly – than any of his predecessors, surviving sculptures of a precious remnant of classical antiquity that was standing (just about) in the middle of a rough-and-ready military base. He would certainly have been able to convince himself that the marbles were safer in his hands (*Illustration 11*).

Almost everything else about Elgin's actions is a matter of speculation, dispute or prejudice. His motives are irrecoverable and were, no doubt, always mixed. He himself wrote nobly, and maybe sincerely, about using the Parthenon and

11. The Parthenon in the second half of the eighteenth century. This engraving from Stuart and Revett's *Antiquities of Athens* gives a slightly romantic tinge to the, no doubt, rather squalid shanty-town which surrounded and encroached on the monument (note the well-tended garden and suspiciously neat peasants). In less than 50 years all the sculpture here visible in the east pediment would be removed by Lord Elgin's agents.

its decoration to encourage the arts and architecture in his native land. All the same, it would be naïve not to suspect a range of more self-seeking ambitions – the kudos of bringing the glories of Greece to Britain among them, and outdoing even Napoleon in the fashionable pursuit of classical treasures. ('Bonaparte has not got such a thing from all his thefts in Italy,' as Elgin was once to boast.) By the end of the story, financial considerations too played a large part. When he finally arranged the sale of the sculpture to the British government in 1816, bankruptcy loomed; servicing his enormous debts must have been uppermost in his mind.

The legal rights and wrongs of the case are just as murky. The actions of Elgin and his agents on the Acropolis were regulated by a firman, a permit detailing what was to be allowed, which was sent by the central government in Constantinople to the local officials in Athens. Did Elgin's men obey or flout the terms of this document? Did they go beyond what they had been allowed to do? The simple answer is that we do not know; and we may well wonder quite how crucial a question it is in our judgement of Elgin anyway (after all, some of the greatest crimes in history have been committed in perfect compliance with the law of the time). None the less, it has prompted interminable modern discussion, spurred on by the tantalising fact that the original firman has never been found, only an Italian translation made for Elgin by the Ottoman court. This Italian version explicitly gives Elgin's men permission to draw, to measure, to put up ladders and scaffolding, to make plaster casts and to dig for what sculptures and inscriptions may lie buried. It is silent on what has always been the main topic of controversy: were they allowed to remove sculpture from the building itself? Is that covered by the instruction in the firman that 'when they wish to take away some pieces of stone with old inscriptions and figures, no opposition be made'? Or are we to assume that what 'they wished to take away' was to include only pieces already fallen to the ground or excavated from the rubble? No amount of poring over the text can provide the answer. As often with documents sent out from head office, the precise interpretation would rest with the men carrying out the orders on the spot. And that would depend on what they imagined the men in Constantinople had in mind, as well as on the usual combination of courtesy, bribery and double dealing that was the hallmark of negotiations between Ottoman officials at Athens and their foreign visitors. It can never have come down to clear, non-negotiable legal limits.

Most commentators at the time were much more ambivalent about Elgin's actions than we usually (thanks to Byron's spin) imagine, and their objections were focused on the prising away of sculpture from the standing remains of the building. They were not generally averse to the idea that Elgin should cart off to Britain the bits and pieces he found by digging or – never mind the villagers – those that were built into the Turkish houses on the Acropolis. Even some of his fiercest critics were playing exactly this game on a smaller scale. Edward Daniel Clarke, for example, a Cambridge polymath who claimed to have observed even the disdar shedding a tear at one of the more brutal bits of intervention in the Parthenon, was not above dealing with the exact same official ('a poor man', as Clarke archly noted) for some choice fragments of Pheidias. In fact, the disdar managed to wheedle out of Elgin's storerooms a precious piece of metope for Clarke to take back to Cambridge. It had been discovered near the entrance to the Acropolis and, as Clarke was later to boast self-righteously, 'it is now in the Vestibule of the University Library at *Cambridge*, a solitary example of sculpture removed from the ruins of the *Parthenon* without injuring what time and the *Goths* have spared'. The joke is that it turned out to be nothing of the sort. Cambridge did not have its own fragment of Pheidias, but a small part of the second-century AD Roman decoration from the nearby Theatre of Dionysus – now in the Fitzwilliam Museum.

The critics' real horror was reserved for the chisels, saws, ropes and pulleys that signalled the dismemberment of the surviving upper levels of the building to extract the sculpture. Dodwell, another eye-witness, rated the 'insensate barbarism' of Elgin's agents even worse than that of the Turks. 'I saw several metopae at the south-east extremity of the temple taken down,' he explained. 'In order to lift them up, it was necessary to throw to the ground the magnificent cornice by which they were covered. The south-east angle of the pediment shared the same fate; and instead of the picturesque beauty and high preservation in which I first saw it, it is now comparatively reduced to a state of shattered desolation.' On the other hand, Dodwell did share enough of Elgin's assumptions about that crucial nexus between art, collecting and patriotism, to concede grudgingly that '… while we indignantly reprove and deeply regret the irreparable damage that has been done to the Athenian monuments, we must not overlook that advantage which the fine arts in our country will derive from the introduction of such estimable specimens of Grecian art'. Even for one of the most strident critics, the issues were more complicated than simple vandalism.

They were also a good deal more political. Scratch the surface of the early nineteenth-century debates about Lord Elgin, and you soon find the competing ambitions of the rival superpowers, Britain and France. The damage done to the Parthenon by Elgin's operations might have been regrettable, but it would have been even worse, in the eyes of many British observers at the time, to see the sculptures falling wholesale into the hands of the French. Byron's long-suffering travelling companion, John Cam Hobhouse, gives us a glimpse of 'the furious struggles … made by both French and English to gain their point'; these were still being fought out when Byron's party arrived in Athens at Christmas 1809. Hobhouse reports a tremendous mixture of tub-thumping jingoism and misinformed rumour. The French deplored the damage and attempted to take the moral high ground, claiming (implausibly) that they were interested only in making plaster casts – not, like Elgin, in snatching the precious originals. For the English, this was just plain sour grapes: 'they only complain because they envy our success, and would themselves have been masters of the same treasures'. Matching tales of French vandalism and megalomaniac schemes quickly followed, as counter-blasts. Choiseul-Gouffier's agents were accused of hacking into the Parthenon to wrench out his metope; this nasty rumour (which was almost certainly false) was apparently being spread by the disdar himself, who may well have found it useful to stir up rivalry between his two main clients. To cap it all, it was said that the French 'even had a plan for *carrying off the whole of the Temple of Theseus!!!*'

For all his friendship with Byron, in the account of his visit to Greece published in 1813 Hobhouse keeps a judicious distance from the various warring sides in this dispute. He holds out little hope for what still survives on the Acropolis ('… if the Turks remain for many more years in possession of Athens, every valuable antiquity will be entirely destroyed'), and he has no truck with scapegoating Elgin ('the fashionable clamour of the day' raised by those 'incapable of appreciating the merit of the remains in question, wherever they may be fixed'). Yet, at the same time, he cannot help but regret that the integrity of the Parthenon has been lost, and he suggests – naughtily in the circumstances – that a Napoleonic conquest of Greece might have given the building as a whole its best chance of proper preservation, 'in the hands of an enlightened enemy'. Among all the scurrilous poems, the pamphleteering, the huffing and puffing for and against Elgin over the last 200 years, this stands out as an unusually careful judgement.

A TEMPLE FIT FOR A KING

Only 10 years or so after the last consignment of Elgin's marbles had left Athens, the Acropolis was a war zone again. It was besieged twice during the War of Independence. First, in 1821–22 when the Turks were forced to surrender to the Greeks for lack of water. Decent terms were agreed, and instantly forgotten. The French consul, Jean-Louis-Sebastien Fauvel (who years earlier had been Choiseul-Gouffier's canny agent in acquiring his Parthenon sculptures) was one of those who did their best to see fair play. But they did not manage to save hundreds of Turks from the Greek knife. In 1826–27, the tables were turned. The Greeks surrendered to the Turks, after a multinational force which had

[94]

come to relieve the siege had been horribly defeated. There was little to choose between the military morals of either side in this conflict.

Inevitably, the Parthenon took some of the punishment – though hardly severe enough to justify any claim by Elgin's supporters that he really had saved the sculpture from complete devastation. Archaeologists have estimated that a further 520 blocks of marble were removed from the temple over this period, for makeshift defences or dismantled for the bullets that could be made out of their lead clamps. One powerful myth of the campaign (elaborated, if not invented, years after) tells of the Greek besiegers sending bullets, as a gift, up to the Turks to prevent them tearing apart any more columns. The sheer boredom of the siege left its mark too. Still visible on photographs of the late nineteenth century are the graffiti scratched on the Parthenon's columns by those penned-up on the Acropolis. One, in particular, captures the romantic imagination, over and above the vicious reality of the fighting on the ground: it read simply 'M Blondel, Philhellene, 1826'. This was the signature, presumably, of a French volunteer who had come to fight for the liberty of Greece – a cause which, as we shall see, would be increasingly symbolised by the very monument on which he scrawled his name.

In the end, the big western powers intervened to impose Greek victory and Greek independence from Ottoman rule. After a failed attempt at a presidency (President Capodistrias was assassinated on his way to church in Nauplion in October 1831; bullets are still carefully preserved in the church wall) and the usual trawl around the minor royalty of Europe, a king was found for the new state in the shape of 17-year-old

Prince Otto, son of King Ludwig of Bavaria. It was an appropriate enough choice, given Ludwig's own passion for classical antiquity, though the lawless, ravaged wasteland that was to be his kingdom can hardly have seemed a particularly attractive inheritance to the Bavarian teenager who disembarked at Nauplion on 6 February 1833 to take up the throne. Athens, it was decided, was to be the capital city, still trading on its historical glamour, despite being now little more than a ruin. A battalion of brightly uniformed Bavarian soldiers moved in to sweep the last surviving Turks off the Acropolis, and to take up residence for a short while in the little Parthenon mosque. Meanwhile, plans were set in motion for transforming the town into a self-respecting European capital, with all the necessary amenities. Two key questions were what to do with the Acropolis and its monuments and where to house the new king.

At this point the history of the Parthenon nearly took one of its most unexpected turns. For back in Bavaria Otto's brother Maximilian got together with his royal friend and amateur architect, Friedrich Wilhelm of Prussia, and came up with the idea of putting the new royal palace on the Acropolis itself; two problems solved at a stroke. For a detailed design, Maximilian commissioned plans from Karl Friedrich Schinkel, the leading Prussian architect and veteran builder of some of the famous landmarks of Berlin (including the Altes Museum and Concert Hall). It was a

12. Schinkel's plan for King Otto's palace on the Acropolis. The distinctive form of the Parthenon can be picked out (lower centre) enmeshed in the labyrinthine structures of the royal residence clustering at the bottom (east) end. The grand entrance to the whole complex, through the ancient Propylaia, is here shown at the top.

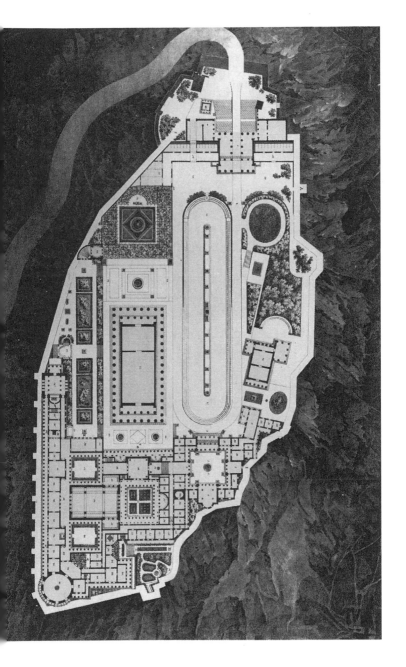

tough brief: create a comfortable, workable and thoroughly modern palace for the new monarchy; make it defensible (it would have been rash, after all, to assume that young Otto's rule would be unchallenged); and incorporate within it the Parthenon and other surviving ancient monuments on site. But Schinkel rose to the task – in a spectacular way, with a design to take over the whole hill (*Illustration 12*). Most of the living quarters were to be concentrated at the east end, an elaborate series of reception rooms, courtyards and shady colonnades, serviced by a network of underground water conduits, backed up by steam-powered pumps if necessary. The main entrance was to be at the west, through the ancient Propylaia and leading up to a huge sunken hippodrome that was to serve as a ceremonial forecourt. Just next to it would be the ruins of the Parthenon itself, standing tall over the rest of the palace, which was carefully planned to be just one storey in height.

For Schinkel's admirers the scheme must have seemed a triumph, a brilliant and tactful combination of the classical past of Greece and its royal present. His critics saw little more than an armchair fantasy by an elderly architect who had never set foot in Athens, and had no idea of the physical or political realities of the place; 'a charming Midsummer Night's dream' as Leo von Klenze, Schinkel's main rival and the architect of the Parthenon-inspired Walhalla, was to dismiss it. For us it is hard to resist the thought that, even if the rest of the palace quarters were planned on a discreet scale, the overall effect would still have been to reduce the Parthenon ruins to a giant folly, a decorative ornament in the royal gardens.

Needless to say, Schinkel's scheme was never built, and

Otto was eventually housed in the lumbering brick mansion that still lines the east side of Syntagma Square. One of the official reasons for rejecting the Acropolis plan was the problem with the water supply (despite Schinkel's ingenious system of conduits and pumps). But other factors certainly weighed: King Ludwig's worries about his son's security and the enormous cost of the project among them. What put paid to the idea most decisively, however, was no practical consideration at all, but a completely different vision of the future of the Parthenon and of the Acropolis as a whole. For another strand of German Hellenism, backed by Schinkel's rival and growing numbers of the new Greek elite, wanted the entire hill to become an archaeological zone and a memorial to the glory days of classical Athens.

THE TRIUMPH OF ARCHAEOLOGY

The Parthenon was officially inaugurated as an ancient monument in an extravagant piece of Bavarian pageantry on 28 August 1834. The ceremony was masterminded by Klenze, who was busy establishing himself as the chief adviser on architecture and archaeology to the royal court. It was to be one of the young king's first official duties. Otto rode on horseback up to the Acropolis, where he was met by the garrison commander and a bevy of Athenian girls, dressed in white and carrying branches of myrtle; one waved a banner blazoned with an image of the goddess Athena, another held a wreath of laurel. As the band played, Otto walked up to the Parthenon itself, where he sat on a throne and, in front of a packed crowd of soldiers, courtiers and local bigwigs, listened politely to a speech delivered by

Klenze in German (translations kindly provided for the Greeks). All around, the detritus of the years of wars, massacre and depredations must still have been horribly visible; just a year earlier, one of the Bavarian soldiers had written of the confused mixture of 'broken pillars, marble blocks, large and small, cannonballs, shell fragments, human skulls and bones' that littered the ground. But Klenze offered a messianic vision of the classical Acropolis 're-born' as the symbol of the new nation-state. 'Your Majesty stepped today', he declared, 'after so many centuries of barbarism, for the first time on this celebrated Acropolis, proceeding on the road of civilisation and glory, on the road passed by the likes of Themistocles, Aristeides, Cimon and Pericles, and this is and should be in the eyes of your people the symbol of your glorious reign … All the remains of barbarity will be removed, here as in all Greece, and the remains of the glorious past will be brought in new light, as the solid foundation of a glorious present and future.' He then asked the king to tap three times on the first column drum of the Parthenon to be restored – and the era of archaeology in the new Greece had begun. Though not archaeology as we know it, perhaps; Klenze's advice was that any material which could neither be reincorporated into the ruins nor made into a picturesque display on the Acropolis should be sold off as building material.

The pageant was a ludicrous piece of theatre but, at the same time, it was an absolutely crucial moment in the history of Greek cultural politics and the archaeology of the Acropolis. Klenze's performance paraded the monuments of the classical Greek past as the most important symbols of the new nation-state. Of course, as we have noted already, earlier generations of Athenians had seen the symbolic potential in their classical heritage; and even before the War of Independence a few Greek intellectuals had called for the preservation of their ancient monuments. But it was the Bavarian monarchy, looking for legitimation and bringing its own traditions of investment in ancient Greek culture, that made the connection between classical antiquities and Greek nationhood absolutely inextricable. As one notable archaeologist put it, speaking to a meeting of the Archaeological Society in Athens in 1838, 'it is to these stones [the sculpture and architecture of classical Greece] that we owe our political renaissance'. This was to become an almost sacred tenet at the heart of Greek national identity, aptly reflected in the popular name that has been given to the Acropolis since the mid-nineteenth century: the Sacred Rock. In due course, it also shifted the terms in which the actions of Lord Elgin were discussed. The early nineteenth-century focus on how much damage was done to the building by the removal of the sculpture still in place was superseded by much more direct appeals to nationalism. If the Parthenon was, as one prominent Greek archaeologist wrote in 1983, 'the most sacred monument of this country ... which expresses the essence of the Greek spirit', then all its sculptures obviously belonged in Greece.

On the Acropolis itself, Klenze's speech heralded a systematic campaign of clearance and excavation. The Bavarian garrison was given its marching orders in 1835 and the site passed into the control of the newly formed Greek Archaeological Service. Over the next 50 years or so, the hill was gradually stripped of virtually all the 'remains of barbarity'. Every trace of the Turkish village was removed, including the minaret on the Parthenon; what was left of the Renaissance palace built into the Propylaia was dismantled; most of the Christian apse in the Parthenon was cleared away; so too was a lot of Roman work, as well as the picturesque Frankish Tower (in fact built by the Florentines) that stood over one corner of the Propylaia and had been a notable landmark on the Acropolis for centuries. At the same time a campaign of excavation went down deeper and deeper through the soil, until there was nothing left but the natural bedrock, exposed over the whole hill-top. By 1890 they could count Klenze's dream fulfilled. As the then director of excavations proudly announced, Greece had 'delivered the Acropolis back to the civilised world, cleansed of all barbaric additions, a noble monument to the Greek genius'.

The present appearance of the site is largely the result of this campaign of clearance and excavation. All that the visitor can now see is what the archaeologists of the nineteenth century chose to leave behind: a handful of monuments with a fifth-century BC classical pedigree, standing in splendid (or uncomfortable) isolation, stripped of as much of their later history as possible. Between them lies the natural rock of the hill. Many visitors take this treacherous, slippery surface to be the ancient ground level. In fact it is nothing of the sort. The ancient Greeks, sensibly, walked on a carefully prepared surface of packed and beaten earth. This bare rock is the product of a vigorous programme of archaeological cleansing and by the standards of today's archaeology a lesson in how *not* to landscape a restored site.

These excavations were, in many respects, an enormous success. They may have been driven by a narrow passion for the Athens of Pericles; but they revolutionised the understanding of the earlier history of the classical buildings on the Acropolis. It became clear, for example, that the Parthenon had not been the first monument on its site. Excavation showed that it had been built on a huge platform which had already held the first few building courses of a partly finished temple, on almost the same scale as the later Parthenon. This 'Pre-Parthenon' was destroyed, just as it was being built, during the Persian invasion of 480 BC – though it has left numerous traces of its brief existence. Some of the marble column drums, cracked by the heat of the fires lit by the Persians, were soon re-used in the north wall of the Acropolis; they were prominently displayed in the defences as if to act as a visible reminder of what the Athenians had sacrificed in the cause of Greek victory. Part of another block, a half-finished column capital, apparently rejected by the original builders in 480 because it had developed a crack, has also been discovered on the site, having spent part of the last two millennia as a door threshold in one of the Acropolis village houses. Many other blocks, we now recognise, were later used in building the Parthenon itself: a signal of prudent economy in a costly project as well as a symbolic reclamation of what the Persians had destroyed.

Over the whole of the Acropolis, the nineteenth-century excavations turned up evidence of its earlier, pre-classical, periods. Many of the most significant finds were soon put on display in a purpose-built museum, carefully constructed to the east of the Parthenon in the 1860s, so as to be almost invisible from the city below – or, indeed, from most of the rest of the site. These included a famous collection of sixth-century BC sculptures, damaged in the Persian invasion and found by the excavators where they had been later buried by the Athenians who came to clear up the wreckage: dozens of stiffly standing maidens with the enigmatic smiling faces characteristic of this period of Greek art, confidently naked youths, a haunting figure of a man carrying a calf. Originally set up on the hill as pious religious dedications or proud displays of individual wealth, they give us some idea of the sheer profusion of images that must have littered the ancient Acropolis.

Also discovered was a series of sculptures from the pediments of temples and other buildings on the Acropolis in the sixth century BC: a magnificent lioness savaging a bull; a still brightly painted monster with a snaky tail and three heads (known affectionately as Bluebeard after the colour of his beards); the goddess Athena dispatching an unfortunate giant; and many others. Here was further crucial evidence for the appearance and layout of the Acropolis over the 100 years or so before the Parthenon was built. But it proved tricky to reconstruct. Even now, despite the confident versions often illustrated in guidebooks to the site or reconstructed in the museum, no one is completely sure which of the sculptures goes with which. 'Bluebeard', for example, has sometimes been put together in the same pediment with the lioness, sometimes not. And there is still less certainty about precisely which buildings any of these reconstructed pediments might have decorated. This is largely because most traces on the ground of the pre-classical structures were removed in later construction work, while the rough-and-ready approach of the archaeologists ensured that any scant hints that did survive until the nineteenth century were carted off in their wheelbarrows, without record. The foundations of one large temple of the 520s BC are still visible between the Parthenon and the Erechtheion; and another is widely thought to have preceded even the Pre-Parthenon (taking the history of temple building where the Parthenon now stands back to about 570). In general, enough material was recovered for us to be fairly confident that the Acropolis was a sacred site for the city of Athens from the very end of the eighth century BC – as far back, that is, as the city (as we know it) had existed. The prehistoric antecedents are another matter. The Acropolis had been settled as early as the second millennium BC, with a Bronze Age Mycenaean palace and a defensive wall that is in places still visible; but whether there was any direct connection between this prehistoric period of occupation and the later religious functions of the site is, frankly, anyone's guess.

While the nineteenth-century excavators were digging down to bedrock, other scholars were busy minutely examining the standing remains of the Parthenon. Now that the garrison village had been cleared away it was much easier to move in and survey the building with all the exactitude that modern technology could offer. One of their particular obsessions was the so-called system of 'optical refinements' deployed in the building's architecture. Parts of this had been observed long before. The English architect C. R. Cockerell, who was in Athens at the very beginning of the century (on his way to acquire the sculptures from the temple of Apollo at Bassae in the Peloponnese), had realised that the columns appeared at a casual glance to taper from bottom to top in a straight line – but in fact, as accurate measurement revealed, bulged slightly in the middle (a trick known in the architectural trade as entasis). Soon after, it was discovered that the columns did not stand exactly perpendicular, as they appeared to the naked eye, but inclined very slightly inwards (modern calculations show that, if they were continued upwards, the columns of the east and west façades would actually meet about 5,000 metres above the floor level). The close observations of the mid-nineteenth century added many other apparent inconsistencies and turned them into a whole system of learned optical illusion. The platform, for example, on which the temple sits (the stylobate) looks to be horizontal; in fact, it curves up in the middle. The columns at the corners are, despite appearances, thicker than those in the middle. And so on.

Generations of modern architectural historians saw these as part of an almost mystical sophistication mastered by the Parthenon's architects. Iktinos and Kallicrates must not only have known, for example, that a truly straight column would appear to the eye to be thinner at the middle, they also knew exactly how to compensate for the visual misapprehension. And such 'refinements' have passed into our own popular mythology of the monument, which is commonly said to be a building 'without any straight lines'. Quite how seriously we should take these arguments is a moot point. It is certainly the case that our major surviving ancient handbook on architecture, by the Roman writer Vitruvius, does recognise a range of optical 'problems' that an architect should be able to correct. But there are other, much more practical, building issues at stake. A stylobate, for example, needs to curve upwards in the middle if it is to allow rainwater to flow off freely. Besides, there is the sneaking suspicion that once a building such as the Parthenon has been acknowledged as a masterpiece, its inconsistencies are always liable to be glorified into a sophisticated optical system – rather than dismissed as the day-to-day improvisations of the builders on site.

One of the most ingenious pieces of detective work ever carried out on the building was the achievement of a young American student at the very end of the nineteenth century. Eugene Andrews had come from Cornell University to the American School of Classical Studies in Athens. As part of his programme he attended a series of Saturday lectures given on site at the Acropolis. On Saturday 7 December 1895 the lecturer concentrated on the east front of the Parthenon. He showed the students a series of marks and cuttings just under the metopes, where at some point in the building's history a row of shields had been fixed right across the façade (the speculation was – probably correctly – that these were gifts of Alexander the Great). Between the ghosts of the shields he picked out another set of cuttings, which marked the fixings of a series of bronze letters; at one time, he explained, an inscription must have been blazoned across the entrance of the temple, but no one had yet worked out what it had said. Andrews took up the challenge. He got permission to rig up a movable platform with a rope ladder (photographs make it look extremely precarious) and he took careful mouldings of each of the groups of letters, using soft wet paper which he left on the building to dry to the shape of the cuttings. He carefully peeled off the paper and took it back to his study to see if he could work out from these fixing holes what the original letters had been.

It turned out to be a nasty surprise. At the very least, even if it was not a remnant of the fifth century, Andrews had anticipated the text would commemorate Alexander and his shields. In fact, as he wrote to his sister, shortly after the decipherment, 'The inscription proved to be a dedication to Nero, whereat I'm much disgusted'. This 'sordid story' was as far as you could imagine from the Periclean Athens that the building had come to symbolise. The 'servile' Athenians, subjects of the Roman empire in the first century AD, must have greeted the arrival in Greece of this notorious emperor in 61 by parading his name in bronze across the entrance of their most famous and sacred building. The most that could be said in mitigation is that they were 'sorry afterwards' for the defacement and quickly removed the offending text (that, at least, was the conclusion he drew from the lack of any obvious weathering around the letters). Andrews never properly published this brilliant discovery. 'I felt no elation', he wrote, looking back in the 1950s, 'at having torn from the Parthenon its shameful secret.'

This overriding preoccupation with the fifth-century Acropolis at the expense of every other historical period had its critics. As almost all the traces of later building were systematically stripped away through the nineteenth century, the (ineffectual) chorus of protest in Greece and overseas grew louder. A particular cause célèbre was the destruction in 1875 of the so-called Frankish Tower that had stood, 27 metres tall, at the corner of the Propylaia. Supporters of its demolition continued to harp on the need to get rid of such 'dark relics of the passing waves of barbarity', while many archaeologists were eagerly expecting that in the debris they would find a treasure trove of inscribed texts, and perhaps sculpture, of the fifth century BC, re-used as building material by the fifteenth-century workmen. Heinrich Schliemann, who could boast of discovering the Homeric city of Troy just a few years before and was now a rich and influential resident of Athens, came up with the money for the demolition work. In fact, not a single inscribed text was found, and waves of dissent spread across Europe, deploring the obliteration of such a well-known landmark. In England E. A. Freeman, historian and father-in-law of that other maestro of prehistoric Greek archaeology, Arthur Evans, penned a tirade for the *Saturday Review* of 21 July 1877. 'It is but a narrow view of the Akropolis of Athens to look on it simply as the place where the great works of the age of Perikles may be seen as models in a museum,' he wrote. 'Only yesterday the tower of the Dukes of Athens was standing … But the tower was late; it was barbarous … We can conceive nothing more paltry, nothing more narrow, nothing more opposed to the true spirit of scholarship, than these attempts to wipe out the history of any age … At all events, let not men calling themselves scholars lend themselves to such deeds of wanton destruction.'

This was all stirring stuff; but it had no effect on official archaeological policy. That did not change until the 1950s, when a longstanding proposal to remove the staircase, in its medieval tower, from the west end of the Parthenon was abandoned once and for all. But by then, more than 100 years after the project of clearance started, the damage had been done. As one historian of Byzantium has recently put it, a visit to the Acropolis today is rather like being taken on a tour around Westminster Abbey, blindfold to everything but the work of Edward the Confessor.

When Virginia Woolf encountered the Parthenon again in 1932, more than 25 years after her first visit, she reflected in her diary on what had changed. 'Yes, but what can I say about the Parthenon – that my own ghost met me, the girl of 23, with all her life to come: that; and then, this is more compact & splendid & robust than I remembered. The yellow pillars – how shall I say? gathered, grouped, radiating there on the rock … The Temple like a ship, so vibrant … It is larger than I remembered, & better held together.' Woolf was righter than she knew. Although her diary entry suggests that she put the changes down to the tricks of memory or the effects of maturity, in the years between her two visits the Parthenon had been substantially rebuilt. It really was 'more splendid & robust … larger & better held together' than it had been in 1906.

For side by side with the policy of clearance and excavation went a sporadic programme of reconstruction of the fifth-century monuments. The most extreme example was the little temple of Victory (Athena Nike), built between 427 and 423 BC, on a parapet high up on the right of the entrance to the Acropolis. This had been completely dismantled by the Turks in 1686 to build defences against the invading forces of the Holy League. It was put together again from scratch immediately after the War of Independence, as the very first major restoration project of the new state. It was taken apart and reassembled again in the 1930s, and is now undergoing its third total reconstruction. In what sense it is the *same* building as that erected 2,500 years ago is very hard to say.

The restoration campaigns on the Parthenon were less radical, but they significantly changed the overall appearance of the building, creating a much less ruined ruin. In 1834, when young King Otto sat on his throne in the temple to listen to Klenze's speech, the building was in its most dilapidated state ever – the clusters of columns at its two ends separated by a vast gaping hole. Through the nineteenth century there were occasional efforts to put some missing sections back in place. In the 1840s, for example, four lost columns in the north colonnade, and one in the south, were partially rebuilt from pieces lying around the site; and 158 blocks were put back on to the walls of the interior rooms, infilling where necessary with modern red brick. But the major interventions came early in the twentieth century, prompted by an earthquake which damaged the building in 1894, as well as by a series of political crises that made an ostentatious investment in the greatest legacy of classical Greece seem a useful piece of public relations. The first round of repairs was finished in 1902; it was relatively modest and was carried out under the aegis of an international committee of advisers who recommended no full-scale reconstruction. But by the 1920s the chief engineer, Nikalaos Balanos, was working effectively without any external supervision and he embarked on a 10-year programme of rebuilding.

This campaign involved all kinds of restoration to the interior walls, strengthening the pediments and reinserting casts of some of the sculpture removed by Lord Elgin. But the most significant change was the re-erection of most of the missing sections of the long colonnades, which had the effect of joining up the east and west ends for the first time since the explosion of 1687. A comparison of the before and

13. The transformation of the Parthenon under Balanos. His finished product (above) certainly looks more impressive than the ruin (below) from which he started. But the iron clamps used in the reconstruction soon threatened to destroy the very marble they were intended to hold together.

after shots in *Illustration 13* gives some idea of the enormous impact of this restoration. At the time there were a few objections to the scale and techniques of this reconstruction. Most people, if they recognised it as reconstruction at all, heartily approved of what Balanos had done. For the building did, as Woolf put it, look considerably more 'splendid', more like a single building, in fact, and a much more fitting approximation to the masterpiece of Periclean Athens that it was supposed to be. It was only much more recently, after Balanos's death and under a new regime of restoration and conservation, that the tide turned against him. It was not just a question of the faint hint of deception that the whole project involved. To be sure, many people do feel uncomfortable that the famous outline of the building, blazoned on postage stamps and tourist posters, was an invention of the 1920s. But there were yet more serious objections to Balanos's methods. First, he made very little attempt to replace blocks in their original position: any column drum would do if it fitted well enough where he wanted it. In this sense his work was nothing like an accurate reconstruction, but a plausible fiction made out of the material he had to hand. Even more crucial, though, was his use of iron rods and clamps throughout the building, inside the ancient marble blocks. In due course this iron oxidised and expanded, splitting open the very masonry it was supposed to be holding in place. Balanos's Parthenon was literally a time-bomb waiting to burst apart.

By the late 1960s the problem of Balanos's iron was compounded by the effects of environmental pollution in Athens, which was steadily eating into the temple's fabric. UNESCO intervened in 1970, with a report which trailed various fantastic solutions for the Acropolis and its monuments (including the idea of encasing the whole hilltop in a perspex bubble). The upshot was the establishment in 1975 of a new committee to supervise the conservation and restoration of all the building on the site. This is now the flagship programme of Greek archaeology, and it proceeds extremely slowly, with exemplary and almost unbelievable care. Every single ancient building block on the Acropolis has been inventoried and measured; rather like hospital patients, each one has its own record card and medical history, its use and re-use over the last three millennia minutely traced. Meanwhile, the overall principles and the detailed proposals for the restoration of each building have been widely discussed in a series of international conferences, which should (if nothing else) deflect some of the criticisms which will inevitably follow. Every intervention is to be reversible. Where a stray block can be replaced in its original position, it will be (that is the best and safest form of conservation). All the sculpture is to be moved from the dangerous open air to the climate-controlled museum – virtually all of it already has been – and will be replaced with exact replicas.

Work started on dismantling and reconstructing the Parthenon itself in 1986. Almost every stone is being lifted out and carefully repositioned. Balanos's iron rods are being removed and replaced with safe (or so we are promised) titanium. Every conceivable expert in the world has been consulted about exactly how many columns to re-erect, and to what height. For the first time ever this is a project with its eyes not only on the building of Pericles, but on the history of the temple, church, mosque and ruin up to the present day.

Although relatively little can be salvaged, the marks of the Venetian cannon-balls and the medieval graffiti are being given no less devoted attention than the fragments of the fifth-century sculpture. When the restoration is finished and visitors can once again (or so it is hoped) walk inside the building that has been closed for so many years, they will be able to see at least a few traces of the twelfth-century church apse, as well as the setting for Pheidias' gold and ivory statue. That is not likely to be much before 2010. When the Parthenon, rebuilt for the twenty-first century, is finally unveiled (and 'rebuilding' is what, in layman's terms, this project is), it will have taken almost twice as long to complete as the original structure of the fifth century BC.

5

'THE GOLDEN AGE OF ATHENS'?

A DEMOCRATIC SPECTACLE

Every evening in Athens during the holiday season hundreds of tourists turn up to one of the longest running pieces of theatre anywhere in the world. It is the Sound and Light show on the Acropolis, inaugurated in 1959 and still well attended by enthusiastic audiences, who watch from a makeshift auditorium on a nearby hillside. As many as 1,500 spotlights are carefully choreographed to pour dazzling colours over the whole hill, or to pick out the individual ruins in turn; while the accompanying soundtrack combines history and fantasy to tell a story of the 'Golden Age of Athens'. The plot is straightforward and dangerously economical with the historical truth: the 'bloodthirsty' Persians come and set fire to the Acropolis (swathed for a few minutes in eerie red light), but the 'courageous' Athenians eventually send them packing and settle down to rebuild their temples and to invent democracy. The hero is Pericles, and selections from his famous 'Funeral Speech', with its stirring slogans about political equality and cultural achievement, make the high point of the crackly voiceover. The whole show is a stalwart relic of one of the mid-twentieth century's most characteristic forms of tourist spectacle, which once illuminated châteaux, cathedrals and castles across western Europe and beyond.

The production at the Acropolis originated in a deal struck between the Greek government and French private enterprise (in the shape of the Son et Lumière Company). Greece gained what was then a state-of-the-art tourist facility and important links with the political mainstream of Europe. The French made money, as well as reasserting their cultural connections with the classical world. On 29 May 1959, 2,500 French sailors marched through Athens on their way to watch the show's première and André Malraux, French Minister of Culture at the time, turned up to give a rousing opening speech. It was a wonderful pageant of Cold War politics, with its celebration of Athens as a bastion of democratic freedom against the evil power of eastern tyranny. But almost 50 years later, the spotlighting of the Parthenon as a symbol of democracy, ancient and modern, still strikes a chord. For the radical (and idiosyncratic) form of popular government developed in fifth-century BC Athens is now more than ever celebrated as the ancestor of western political freedom: 'our' democracy, we have come to believe, has its ideological origins in Athens. And the Parthenon, as one of the acknowledged masterpieces of fifth-century culture, can stand as a visible guarantee of the virtues of democracy (both theirs and ours).

Like all such myths, this particular myth of democratic Athens is true in parts. During the fifth century, a series of reforms did progressively remove political privilege from the aristocratic elite of the city. Ultimate authority was vested in the assembly of all citizens who took the important decisions of state at open meetings and rigorously scrutinised the conduct of state officials. These officials were not elected; for elections, so the logic went, were always liable to be swayed by wealth or influence or training. The vast majority were selected randomly by lot to give every citizen an equal chance of political office. Frequent rotation of office made sure that anyone who was keen had plenty of opportunity to be involved; and financial compensation was provided (thanks in part to the profits of empire) so that no one was prevented by poverty from participating. The main exceptions to this rule were the generals, who continued to be chosen by election (and might even be elected, as Pericles was, year after year). Even an ultra-democrat would have been loth to entrust Athenian fortunes in battle to whomsoever the lottery happened to throw up; the democracy was not so narrowly ideological as to put its equal-opportunities policy before the state's survival.

It was an extraordinary experiment in popular government. Predictably, all kinds of questions have been raised by modern historians about exactly how it worked. Every citizen could in theory participate in the political process; but how far did they? And what counted as participation? Some critics have pointed out that the place where the assembly regularly met was hardly geared to mass involvement, since it could only accommodate a small proportion, not much more than 10 per cent, of those eligible to attend. Others have interpreted participation more generously: if you take into account not just the assembly but all the different forms of political and public service (from the local government of the various city wards and outlying villages to the legal courts which brought in thousands of citizens as jurors), then the vast majority of citizens must have been actively involved. Some have stressed the effective power of the lottery in overcoming the discrepancies of birth, wealth and privilege.

Others have cynically noted that, lottery or not, all the key political figures in the fifth century, those whose names we know, were rich – and many, like Pericles, came from the traditional landed aristocracy whose political privileges had ostensibly been removed by the democratic reforms. But, however you choose to resolve these particular debates, the fundamental principle that sovereignty lay with the people (the *demos*, in Greek) defined Athenian political identity in the fifth-century world: Athens was a *demokratia*.

That said, those who would now idealise it as a symbol of democracy for the modern world must turn a blind eye to some of its (to us) less congenial aspects. Crucially the *demos*, the group of citizens who shared in the democratic government of Athens, made up only about 50,000 of a total population that lay somewhere between 300,000 and 400,000, or so our best estimates for the mid-fifth century, immediately before the Great War with Sparta, would suggest. Completely excluded from political rights were women, children and perhaps as many as 100,000 slaves. So too was anyone, Greek or not, who was of non-Athenian blood ('resident aliens', as we might now call them). Pericles himself was responsible for tightening up the criteria for full citizenship, successfully piloting legislation in 451 BC to rule out anyone who did not have *both* an Athenian mother *and* an Athenian father; previously just an Athenian father had been enough. It would, of course, be perversely anachronistic to invest too much disapproval in the exclusion of women and slaves. On those terms almost every political regime before the mid-nineteenth century would be more or less deplorable (though the Athenian version of misogyny looks bad even by ancient standards). But the inescapable fact is that the Athenian democracy delivered political equality only to a privileged cadre of the city's inhabitants, and one which was ethnically and culturally homogeneous. Seen in this light, it seems an unpromising model for today's open, ethnically diverse and multicultural attempts at democratic government.

It is also an inescapable fact that democracy was bitterly contested within Athens itself. The popular romantic image of the Athenian Golden Age pictures a community united in its struggles against the barbarians and in its eagerness to forge a new political order; it is an image of democratic consensus. But the reality was nothing of the sort. There were always a few Athenians tempted to throw in their lot with the Persians (and, ironically, by the last decades of the fifth century both Athens and Sparta saw Persian financial backing as the key to victory in their Great War). There were even more to whom the democracy seemed a pernicious mistake. The reforms which devolved increasing power to the *demos* were not passed without a fight, and there were times in the fifth century when the democratic system survived only by the skin of its teeth. Indeed, at a low point in the war against Sparta, pressure from the opposition led to the temporary suspension of democracy, and its replacement by an oligarchy which gave political rights to just 5,000 men. Pericles, as we have seen him on stage in the 'Funeral Speech', must have needed all the spin he could muster in support of his democratic principles. In fact, what may well be the oldest work of Greek prose literature to survive (we have poetry from much earlier) is a ranting political pamphlet from fifth-century Athens written by an implacable, if rather muddled, opponent of the democracy; and Pericles' most influential political partner was actually assassinated in the late 460s after he had contrived the removal of one of the last bastions of aristocratic privilege. This seedier side of Athenian political life is rarely glimpsed in such rosy-tinted visions of democracy as are projected in the Sound and Light show, and in other popular celebrations of what has been called the 'Greek Miracle'.

In order to understand the classical Parthenon, we need to bridge the gap between the familiar reconstructed ruin – floodlit on the Acropolis, visited by millions, celebrated across continents – and its ancient prototype; and to think more carefully about the relationship of the fifth century's most famous icon to the politics, culture and religion of the society that created it. There is, as we shall see, a world of difference between the glamorous allure of 'Periclean' Athens that dominates our vision of the monument and the sometimes surprising history of the temple that is revealed by archaeology. It is a history that starts with the ambitious building schemes of the mid-fifth century, but continues in a whole series of repairs, adaptations and 'improvements' through the hundreds of years of Greek and Roman antiquity that followed.

TREASURE TROVE

The Acropolis was crammed with sculpture, dedications, memorabilia and bric-à-brac of all sorts. Pausanias himself confessed to be spoiled for choice in picking out the highlights for his readers' attention. By contrast, his description of the Parthenon itself seems strikingly spare: focusing on the gigantic statue of the goddess Athena, he notes only the sculpture in the pediments and a couple of portrait statues inside. But we should not be misled by Pausanias' silence. As soon as it was built, the interior of the Parthenon was an Aladdin's cave of treasure — and junk.

The plan of the building gives no hint of this at all (*Figure 5*). It shows the familiar simple design of Greek temple architecture: an outer circuit of columns surrounding a plain internal chamber (in fact here — and this was an unusual feature of the Parthenon — *two* internal rooms). The main entrance at the east led into the larger room, where the great gold and ivory statue loomed. Around the room on three sides ran a two-storey colonnade, one tier of columns supporting another. At some point after the building was finished (we do not know exactly when) a shallow pool of water was installed in front of the statue. Referring back to this feature at another point on his travels, Pausanias explains that the idea was to increase the humidity and so prevent the ivory drying out. But the pool must also have served to reflect the light entering the room from the east, through the main door and through the room's only two windows which were set high up on the east wall. It was from this end too that you could get access to the roof, by a stairway hidden in the thickness of the wall. Architectural historians have wrangled for almost 200 years about how this roof was constructed (almost nothing was left in place after the 1687 explosion). One favourite nineteenth-century theory was that it was open to the sky at the centre. They had not yet realised that there had been windows in the east wall, and this was a convenient solution to the problem of how these rooms were originally lit. Convenient it may have been, but, as every modern study now agrees, it was also wrong. There was, it seems, a full roof of marble tiles, supported by wooden rafters.

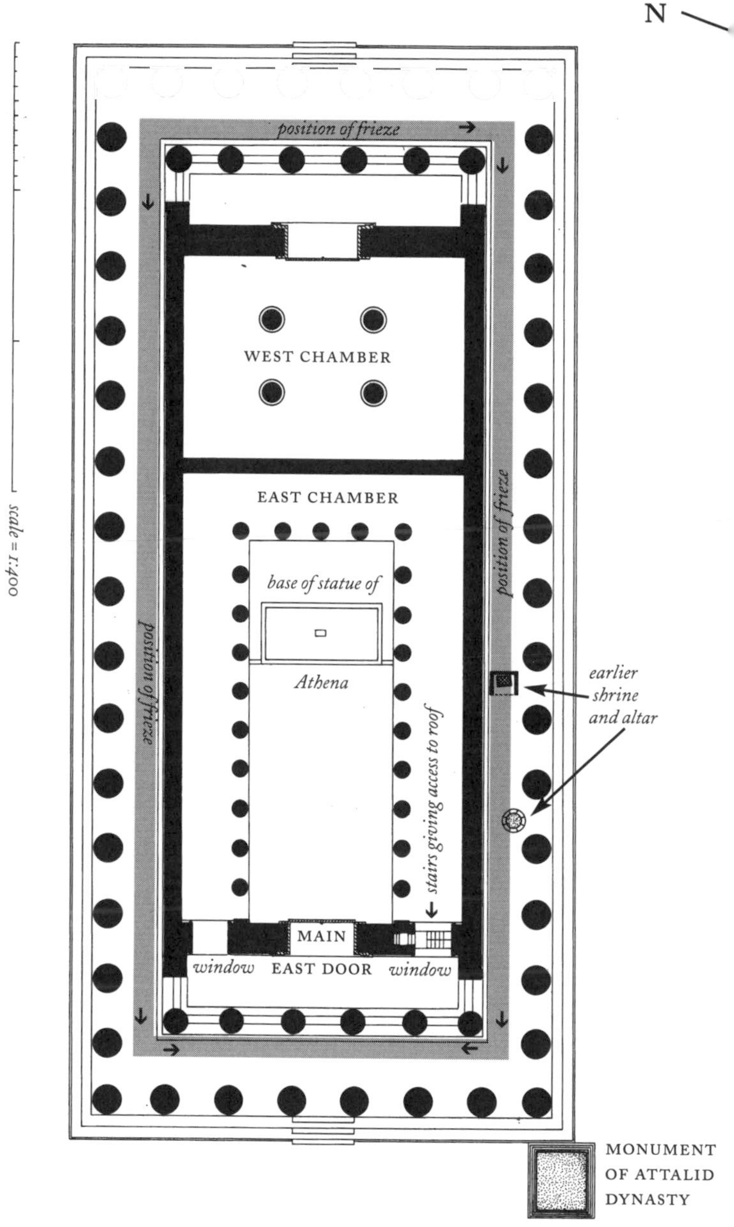

N

scale = 1:400

position of frieze

position of frieze

position of frieze

WEST CHAMBER

EAST CHAMBER

base of statue of

Athena

stairs giving access to roof

MAIN

window EAST DOOR *window*

earlier
shrine
and altar

MONUMENT
OF ATTALID
DYNASTY

Figure 5. Plan of the ancient Parthenon.

There was no connection between the eastern and western rooms; not, at least, until the three doors were opened up by the Christians to give access between what became their foyer (or narthex) and the main sanctuary of the church to the east. During the classical period the western chamber could be entered only by its own external door. Its main feature was the group of four single columns rising in the centre – and, in contrast to where the statue stood, the murky gloom. This smaller room really does seem to have had no windows at all.

But the outline plan is only part of the story. We can fill in many other crucial details thanks to some of the most revealing documents ever found on the Acropolis. These are fragments of a series of inventories of the Parthenon's contents, originally drawn up by the Treasurers of Athena (the state officials who managed and audited the goddess's property), then inscribed on stone and put on public display. They were intended presumably not only as a record of the temple's holdings, but also as a guarantee of the probity of the men who managed them. The surviving texts start just after the Parthenon's construction and run to the end of the fourth century BC (when the administrative system seems to have changed). They give us a vivid picture of the building piled high with sacred property of all kinds, dedications rich and humble, the city's heirlooms and the wealth of the goddess herself. In 434/3, for example, when the temple was only just being finished, in the front porch alone were stored 113 silver bowls (plus one in gold) for use in sacrifices, three silver drinking horns, three silver cups, a silver lamp and a small goblet in a box. The eastern chamber itself, alongside the statue of Athena, could boast three golden bowls (large ones, to judge by their recorded weights), a golden statue of a woman and a silver basin. The dark western room was the most crowded storehouse of all, counting among its much longer list of treasures six Persian daggers, one gilt lyre (plus three in ivory and four in wood), an ivory inlaid table, a silver-gilt mask, 10 couches from Miletos, six thrones, two large silver-gilt nails, and over 70 shields. Some of this looks like war booty or state valuables; some like the religious paraphernalia that any cult might need. But some must have been the result of private offerings. Later records in fact sometimes note the name of person who gave the object in question. These range from a small ivory figurine of a cow dedicated by a woman called Smikythe in the 370s, or a simple gold ring offered by Dorkas, 'a foreigner living in Piraeus', to the no doubt much more splendid (and pricier) golden drinking horn presented to Athena by Roxane – none other, as the text insists, than the wife of Alexander the Great.

The Parthenon was, as one archaeologist has recently put it, a 'strongbox'. It held the treasures owned by the goddess, which in practice were not always easy to distinguish from the property of the state. Certainly, towards the end of the Great War against Sparta some of the precious dedications were melted down in aid of the war effort, and it was presumably with such circumstances in mind that Pheidias is said to have ensured that the gold panels on the statue of Athena were easily detachable (the Athenians resisted this particular temptation throughout the fifth century, but the gold plates are supposed to have been used to pay troops during civil war in the third century BC). The presence of all these valuables makes a huge difference to how we envisage the appearance of the Parthenon, its day-to-day use and, inevitably, its policing.

Storage and security must have been near the top of the agenda. The bare walls shown on the plan were covered with cupboards and shelf-stacks (each carefully numbered, so the inscriptions suggest), and chests littered the floor. To protect the treasures kept in the porches, barriers or grilles were fixed between the inner row of columns at both east and west ends; the cuttings for these are still clearly visible. Far from our usual image of an open building, what actually faced visitors as they walked up the steps towards the doorway of the main eastern chamber was a metal fence. How their access into the building was controlled we do not know. Pausanias mentions no difficulty in getting inside when he visited in the second century AD. But it is impossible to imagine that such a store of valuables could have been accessible to the general public without a substantial presence of warders and guards (much like today); and when the staff were off-duty, the Parthenon – maybe even the whole Acropolis – must have been securely locked and bolted. It is also impossible to imagine, given the clutter of contents, that the Parthenon could have been used for anything much other than the display of the goddess's statue and the storage of valuables. That would not make it unusual among Greek temples. These were not, in general, designed to hold a congregation and were not seen as places of communal worship. In ancient Greece, religion was much more of an open-air event; the key ritual of animal sacrifice took place around an outdoor altar. The temple's principal job was to house (the statue of) the deity. It was not for centuries, until the Parthenon became a church and then a mosque, that it functioned as a religious building in the sense with which we are familiar. Indeed, those who later so admired the single golden dove circling over the altar of Our Lady of Athens, the everlasting lamp and St Luke's icon of the Virgin would never have believed what treasures had once been crammed into their church.

MAKING SENSE OF THE FRIEZE

No less remarkable was the sheer quantity of sculpture which originally decorated the Parthenon. Greek temple architecture is a classic combination of rigid conservatism and subtle innovation. All temples did look broadly the same (they were presumably intended to be instantly recognisable). Yet, at the same time, their architects were always improvising, or bending the conventions, to create something new; no one temple is, after all, exactly identical to any other. The Parthenon bends many more conventions than most, and none more strikingly than in its repertoire of sculpture. True, there were plenty of precedents in older temples across the Greek world for a frieze running around the building, for sculpted metope panels and statue-laden pediments – as well as for the skyline figures (probably, in this case, huge statues of the goddess Victory) that perched at the four corners of the roof. But no designers had ever before deployed all these together on the same building; no designers had ever produced a temple quite so heavily decorated. Indeed, even here, the sculpted frieze seems not to have been part of the original plan. Architects working on the recent restoration programme have found clear evidence that in its first design the building featured just a row of metope panels over the east and west entrances, where the frieze now runs; only later in the project was this replaced by the much more ambitious complete frieze. It is a telling indication of how the building scheme must have developed 'on the job'. It is also a hint of some of the other surprises about the Parthenon's design and original appearance which have been sprung, as we shall shortly see, by the restorers' minute analysis of every cubic millimetre of the building's fabric.

Of all the sculpture that once loaded the building it is the frieze that is always the most keenly discussed, largely because (unlike much of the rest) it survives reasonably intact; about 128 metres of its original length of 160 are preserved in either London or Athens (plus Choiseul-Gouffier's fragment in the Louvre). It shows a procession, which starts out at the south-west corner of the building and makes its way, in two halves (one down the south side, one round the west and then down the north), to the main entrance into the Parthenon. Horsemen, charioteers, musicians, water-carriers, animals for sacrifice all converge, from their two sides, on a strikingly enigmatic climax which is shown directly over the eastern door itself (*Illustration 14*): a piece of cloth is held up by, or passed between, a man and a child (male or female, it is not clear); behind the man, a woman seems about to take more cloth, or perhaps padded stools, from a pair of girls; on either side a group of deities, 12 in all, sit with their backs to the scene – recognisably superhuman, because even seated they equal the height of the standing mortals.

Art historians are almost unanimous in their admiration for this frieze and, especially, for its brilliant handling of depth and perspective. The carving is extraordinarily shallow, never more than six centimetres from the front surface of the marble to the back; and yet the sculptors have still managed

14. The puzzle at the centre of the Parthenon frieze. Is this the ceremonial presentation of the new robe (or *peplos*) for Athena? Or the eerie preliminaries to a tragic human sacrifice?

15. Part of the calvacade of young cavalrymen who are so prominent in the frieze. These two riders are busy reining in their horses; the holes where metal harnesses would originally have been fitted are still just visible on the horses' heads.

to represent convincingly teams of horses sometimes as many as four deep. They also seem to have taken account of the awkward position of the viewer, who would necessarily be standing a good 12 metres below the sculpture and looking up at a very sharp angle. The carving is consistently deeper at the top of the panels than at the bottom so that the figures actually lean outwards; the idea was, presumably, that this would make them clearer to see from below. But the un-animity ends with the technique. When it comes to the subject matter, there are any number of different views about how we should understand the scenes depicted on the frieze and how they relate to the rest of the monument and to Athenian culture more generally. In this sense, it has become one of the longest running puzzles in the whole of classical art history. A wry reflection might put this down, paradoxi-cally, to its excellent state of preservation. For here (as else-where in the history of classical art and culture) the more that survives, the more we are forced to face the sheer complexi-ties of interpretation.

Few people can resist projecting their own version of fifth-century Athens on to this particular work of art. For some, the youthful naked riders key into the well-known homoeroticism of classical Athenian culture (*Illustration 15*). For others, uncanny similarities between the frieze and the sculptures from the palace façades at the Persian capital of Persepolis hint at an aggressive attempt to appropriate the artistic forms of the enemy. Others have struggled to relate the frieze to the city's democratic ideology. Assuming that the procession is an image of the Athenian polity itself, they see the striking uniformity of the faces and expressions as an idealising version of the city's democratic principles, subordinating individual distinction and prestige to the common good. Yet they puzzle over the unexpected and disproportionate prominence of the cavalry. In the mid-fifth century the cavalry made up only a tiny proportion of the city's fighting force (perhaps little more than 1,000); it was one of the few surviving bastions of the aristocratic rich. So why do these heroic and gloriously youthful horsemen dominate this flagship monument of the democracy? It is a hint perhaps of the elitism that (paradoxically to us) lay at the heart of the Athenian democracy's self-image.

The bitterest arguments focus on what are apparently the simplest questions: what does the frieze show? what particular occasion, idea or myth, is here cast into stone? The earliest travellers to Athens made some brave conjectures. Cyriac of Ancona, for example, reckoned it was a display of Athenian victories at the time of Pericles (fine for the cavalry and chariots maybe, harder to align with the water carriers and cows, let alone the decidedly unmilitary central scene). But most modern discussions of the theme of the frieze kick off from an inspired guess by James Stuart, published in the *Antiquities of Athens* in 1789. His clever idea was that it showed the procession of the so-called 'Panathenaic festival', which came up to the Acropolis every year, bringing with it a new robe (or *peplos*) for the ancient image of Athena; not the gold and ivory version in the Parthenon (which played, so far as we can tell, no part at all in the city's regular rituals), but a much older and plainer sacred image of the goddess, made of olive wood, and by the end of the fifth century housed just opposite the Parthenon in the shrine known as the Erechtheion (see *Figure 3*). This offered an irresistibly neat solution to the puzzling scene at the climax of the procession,

16. One guess at how the east pediment might have been arranged. In this relatively sedate version Zeus (who has just given birth) stands in the centre, flanked on the right by his wife Hera and on the left by the new-born Athena. The horse of the moon (*Illustration 16*) is to the far right; the figure of Theseus/Hercules (*Illustration 20*) reclines on the opposite side, next to the horses of the sun.

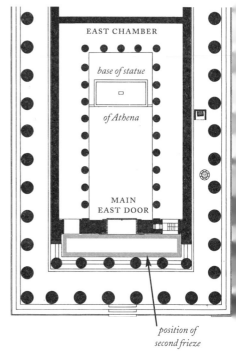

position of second frieze

Figure 6. Position of the second frieze (shaded).

for, if this was the Panathenaic procession, the strange bundle of cloth was obviously the *peplos* for the statue. Even 200 years later, some version of Stuart's explanation of the frieze still seems the best on offer to many people.

Yet there are problems. If this is meant to be the Panathenaic procession, then why are some of its most characteristic features missing? Where, for example, is the distinctive ship-on-wheels which transported the new *peplos* through the city, spread out like a sail? And why so many horsemen, when the literary accounts stress the ranks of foot-soldiers who marched with the procession? Besides, how do we explain why the Athenians broke what seems otherwise to have been an iron rule of Greek temple sculpture – that only mythological scenes, and never events from real life, were represented? Enough doubts have always been raised to keep open the whole question of what exactly the frieze was about. And occasionally entirely new 'explanations' are touted, which often enjoy a few years of scholarly favour in turn before fading away. The most celebrated (or notorious) include an ingenious exercise in numerology, which made the frieze a memorial to a glorious Athenian victory against the Persians by calculating that the total number of participants in its procession was equal to the number of Athenians killed at the Battle of Marathon (the trouble was that it required some rather creative counting to reach the magic figure of 192). Most recently, and no less ingeniously, it has been argued that the frieze has nothing to do with the Panathenaic procession at all, but depicts a famous incident in Athenian mythology, when the legendary king Erechtheus sacrificed his daughter to save Athens from invasion. On this view the indeterminate child at the climactic scene must be a girl; she is holding not the goddess's *peplos*, but her own shroud, and the other girls are her sisters, shrouds in hand, all ready to follow suit.

These bright new ideas for the subject of the frieze are often proposed with tremendous verve and learning. Yet none of them has ever quite succeeded in burying the theory of James Stuart. More to the point, it is hard not to feel that 'spotting the theme', in this narrow sense, is something of a dead-end. How, after all, would we recognise the correct 'solution' if we found it? Is the absence of the ship-on-wheels, for example, or the foot-soldiers, conclusive evidence that we are not dealing with the Panathenaic procession? Do we really expect an artistic representation of any event to be a literal transcription of it? How could we ever prove that the child with the 'shroud' was meant to be a girl, not a boy?

In fact, a salutary warning of the fragility of the whole exercise has been sounded by what is perhaps the most surprising discovery of any made in the course of the recent restoration. For we now know that there was not just one, but two, friezes on the fifth-century Parthenon, a second whose existence no archaeologist had ever before suspected. 'Our' frieze ran above the inner columns at east and west, and around the outside walls of the two interior rooms (*Figure 2*). This 'new' frieze ran at the same level around the inner eastern porch and directly above the main eastern door (*Figure 6*). It was much shorter and only faint traces survive; it seems to have been largely destroyed by a devastating fire in the third century AD and then almost completely removed in the repair work that followed. But just about enough has survived to show that it was in deeper relief than the outer frieze and that, at one point, it featured a row of standing female figures. The implications are tantalising. Whatever this frieze depicted, it would have been clearly visible, beyond the outer frieze, to any visitor climbing the steps to the main entrance of the building; it is almost bound to have been seen as the continuation of the narrative which ended (or so, up till now, we have believed) at the scene with the *peplos* or shroud. Nothing more can be known (though it is a fair bet that the next 50 years will see a whole range of imaginative 'reconstructions'). But it is an unsettling thought that the premise on which almost every explanation of 'our' frieze has always been based – that the strangely low-key incident with the cloth marks the climax of the story – is now called into question.

THE EYE OF FAITH

Much of the rest of the original sculpture is pitifully ruined. Leaving aside the great statue of Athena, which we now know only as a wonderful fantasy (pp. 28, 40–41), loosely based on Pausanias' description and the multitude of ancient 'replicas' and souvenirs, archaeologists are still hard at work piecing together the sculpture from the pediments and the metopes; and significant fragments are still turning up on the Acropolis and in museum basements. For modern visitors to the British Museum or to Athens, the sculptures from the pediments require the eye of faith. Only a few have survived well enough to give some idea of the original quality of the work. The head of the exhausted horse (*Illustration 17*) which once nestled into the far right-hand corner of the east pediment (featuring the birth of Athena) has always been a popular favourite. The extreme angles of the pediment

17. The horse of the Moon from the east pediment. Generations of visitors to the British Museum have enthused over this brilliant representation of sheer weariness: its flaring nostrils and jaw drooping over the edge of the pediment. Others, more recently, have wondered quite how much damage was done to its delicate surface in a notorious programme of cleaning in the 1930s (pp. 168–73).

triangle were a tricky challenge for the classical sculptor. How could you fill this tiny cramped space with any figure that was plausibly in scale with the characters who occupied the centre-ground? Dead bodies were, predictably perhaps, a common choice. Here the design offers something quite new. This tired horse drives the chariot of the Moon down below the horizon, as it sinks beneath the pediment floor, while in the other angle the horses of the Sun are just rising. Athena's birth, in other words, finds its place in a cosmic scheme: it happened *at* dawn, just as the moon was setting and the sun coming up, and it *was* a new dawn, in all kinds of other senses, for Athens and for humanity. By and large, however, the battered, eroded and, for the most part, headless figures tend to baffle, rather than excite, most viewers.

The game of restoration consists in trying to match up Pausanias' identification of the subject matter of the pediments (east: birth of Athena; west: contest between Athena and Poseidon) with the drawings produced before the explosion of 1687 for the Marquis de Nointel and with the fragments of sculpture that still survive. Without the drawings, it would now be next to impossible to get any overall idea of how the pediments were arranged. But even with them, crucial problems remain. We have no idea at all how the birth of Athena itself was depicted, for the central figures over the main east entrance had disappeared long before the Marquis de Nointel arrived, when the building was first converted to a church. Was she really shown literally popping out of Zeus' head, as the myth had it – and as is sometimes found in smaller-scale depictions of the story? Or was it, as many scholars now guess, a more prosaic, less obstetric rendering, with Athena calmly standing next to her father Zeus (though hardly a 'birth' in Pausanias' terms) (*Illustration 16*)? There has also been, and still is, tremendous disagreement about who all the other figures in each pediment were meant to represent. The gamut of Olympian deities and local Athenian heroes has been canvassed, as well as a good number of more unlikely candidates. In fact, in the eighteenth century, two of the figures that still survived on the west pediment were widely assumed to be later additions: portraits of the Roman emperor Hadrian and his wife Sabina, strategically inserted, so people then assumed, into a group of bona fide Greek gods (much as Nero's name had been blazoned across the façade). It was, almost certainly, a crashing misidentification; they are now usually thought to be some mythical Athenian king and his daughter. But it was a misidentification that kept them in Athens; for Elgin's agents did not consider a pair of Romans to be worth all the trouble of removing and transporting back to England.

Not all the metope panels are in such a frustrating condition. A group of around 20 from the south side of the building are, for some unknown reason (p. 57), well preserved. They show scenes from the famous mythical brawl at the wedding feast of the King Pirithous, which was rudely interrupted by a gang of monstrous centaurs who had come to carry off the girls. Some of these surviving panels are virtuoso displays of artistic expertise (*Illustration 18*). But others, including several in Elgin's collection and Choiseul-Gouffier's prize possession, have fascinated art historians precisely because they are frankly second-rate. Take, for example, the panel shown in *Illustration 19*. Despite the occasional valiant attempt to defend its extremely awkward rendering of both centaur and Greek, it is hard to resist the conclusion that the sculptor was really not up to the job; that he did not leave himself enough room to give the centaur even the hint of a neck; and that he produced a feeble Greek fighter with one leg demonstrably longer than the other.

These rather clumsy efforts hint at the problems that must have faced those who were managing the Parthenon project as a whole. We have no idea who exactly these managers were. Many modern scholars have been tempted to follow Plutarch and to see the famous sculptor Pheidias as the artistic (and organising) genius behind the whole sculptural programme; though others have thought it more realistic to imagine that he was involved only with the great statue of Athena. But one thing is certain: even if Pheidias did devise the grand plan, he could not possibly have had the time to lay his chisel on more than a tiny proportion of the marble. Huge numbers of trained sculptors would have been needed to get through the work on what was clearly a tight schedule; on the frieze, for example, as many as 80 different hands have been detected. Where was this workforce to be found? In the schedule of operations, the metopes were the first sculptures on the list. It seems very likely that, at this stage, the project manager (Pheidias or not) was forced to turn to the untrained, the time-expired, the less-than-talented or the young. Later, perhaps, training and recruitment went more smoothly. Certainly neither the work on the frieze nor (so far as we can tell) that on the pediments shows any such variety of style or skill, despite the numbers of sculptors involved.

For most of the metopes, however, quality is no longer an issue; as we saw (p. 55), they were defaced almost beyond recognition when the temple was converted to a church. To

18. One of the most spectacular of all the metope panels. A centaur tries to escape (putting his hand to a wound in his back), while the young Greek prepares to deliver a fatal blow. This metope stretches the idea of relief sculpture to its limits. The figure of the Greek stands almost entirely free of the background marble.

19. Frankly second rate? The contrast with *Illustration 18* (which would have been its neighbour on the Parthenon itself) is striking. Perhaps the juxtaposition was intentional and the designer was trying to parade different versions of bestiality with this awkwardly neckless centaur. More likely it was a less competent job by a less competent sculptor.

judge from what was left after this chiselling, they all seem to have shown scenes of mythical battles: the northern side, Greeks versus Trojans; the west, Greeks versus the legendary women fighters, the Amazons; the east, gods versus the giants who once upon a time tried to usurp their position on Mount Olympus. In many ways, this is the standard repertoire of Greek temple sculpture; but the sheer insistence here on these myths of Greek victory, and the repeated variations on the theme through different legendary cycles, key into the idea of the Parthenon as a monument of Athenian triumph. The defeat of the Persians, whose shields and daggers were to be found amongst the war booty in the storeroom below, is here figured in terms of the most powerful cultural axioms of the Athenian fifth century: men defeat women, Greeks conquer foreigners, gods triumph over their enemies, civilisation prevails over monstrosity. Several of these motifs were picked up and replayed inside the building too (part of an elaborate 'Pheidian' design, as some would see it). The edges of Athena's sandals paraded another version of Greeks versus centaurs, battles of Greeks and Amazons were found again on the outside of her shield, while painted, or perhaps inlaid, on its inner surface was the victory of gods over giants. In fact, as if to assert the links between sculpture and ritual, that victory of gods over giants also formed the standard motif of the elaborate woven *peplos* made each year for the ancient image of Athena, the *peplos* which itself may (or may not) have been cast in stone in the frieze above the entrance of the Parthenon.

But the Parthenon was not a sculpture gallery. True, many of the sculptures that once decorated it have long taken their places in the roster of museum masterpieces. Right back to antiquity they have been admired and discussed as 'works of art'. And the building itself has been equally lionised in the story of world architecture (thanks in part, no doubt, to the self-advertising treatise by its designer Iktinos). Yet it was also a highly charged piece of sacred space. It makes a tremendous difference to the way we understand the fifth-century monument if we put religion – and specifically Athena – back into the frame.

Jewish and Christian polemic worked hard and very successfully to ridicule 'paganism' (as Christians called it). Even now we tend to picture the different gods and goddesses that defined Greek and Roman polytheism in the terms that their opponents chose: a range of larger-than-life characters, with dubious morals, family tensions worthy of a soap opera and a range of mythical powers usually used (like thunderbolts) irresponsibly and to the disadvantage of mankind. This was a wilful misrepresentation. Polytheism was much more nuanced and complex than its monotheistic critics saw, or wanted to let on. Good romping stories of divine peccadillos were only part of the picture. The point was that the range of divinities, their different characteristics, responsibilities and family relationships represented an ambitious attempt to classify the world, to explain (and dispute) the nature of power and social relations, to understand the universe and humanity's place in it. Athena, for example, was not simply 'the goddess of wisdom' as she appears, briskly defined, in modern encyclopaedias; she embodied a particular kind of 'cunning intelligence' (the word *metis* in Greek has no easy English translation) that played a part in such varied activities as carpentry, warfare, statecraft and weaving. The lurid story of her birth directly from the head of her father Zeus, who had swallowed her mother, the goddess Metis, was one way of picturing how that quality was controlled, shared and passed down in the divine order of things.

It was a religious system that dealt in questions, myths and metaphors rather than in creeds and the tenets of belief (hence, perhaps, the puzzlement of so many Christian critics). One of the questions at the very top of the religious agenda was the nature of divinity itself: what were the gods like? How did they intervene in human affairs? How would you recognise them? In what ways were they different from, or similar to, humankind? All kinds of answers were improvised in philosophical treatises, in myth, and in drama; but artists had a particularly privileged role in (literally) making likenesses of the gods for their community. The most loaded and influential images of all were those images which stood *as the gods* inside their temples. Different kinds of statues played to different versions and interpretations of divine nature and appearance.

So far, we have written off Pheidias' enormous gold and ivory version of Athena as a rather vulgar creation, extremely precious but difficult to admire (frankly better lost, some have thought). But we will think of it differently if we take it not just as an extravagant piece of display, but as an attempt to capture the nature of divinity. For, as well as an expensive masterpiece, it was also a *way of seeing* the goddess. Some of the commonest claims made by Greek writers were that deities were much larger than humans and shone with a dazzling radiance. Pheidias here has instantiated just those ideas, with his colossal, shiny, polished image of Athena. It was an image that was so precious that it must have been mostly off-limits, visible yet untouchable to all but the favoured few.

But Pheidias devised this image of Athena in close (and significant) proximity to a quite different representation of the goddess. The old statue of Athena kept next door in the Erechtheion and dressed each year in the new *peplos* was, it seems, little more than an olive-wood plank – albeit decked out with all kinds of jewellery. Its sacred status came not from the immense skill and cost with which some first-rate artist had conjured up for humanity a likeness of the deity, but from its extreme antiquity, its resolute refusal to ape human form in any detail and the story (as retold at least by Christian critics) that it was not made by human hand at all, but had fallen miraculously to earth from the heavens. It was a divine creation, surrounded by mystery – but at the same time old and familiar, lovingly cared for, washed, tended, adorned and dressed (with the *peplos*) by groups of women in the city.

These are two radically different ways of imagining the goddess. And the Parthenon prompted its visitors to notice and to compare them. Anyone who entered the temple to marvel at Pheidias' version of Athena must necessarily have passed directly beneath the scene in the frieze which alludes (on many interpretations, at least) to the cult of the old olive-wood image; that is to say, as they were about to enter the inner room and to wonder at the colossal gold and ivory goddess, they would have seen above them the preparation of the *peplos* for the *other* statue. Meanwhile, another recent discovery made during the restoration programme may reinforce the importance of these two different versions of sacrality. The north colonnade of the Parthenon turns out not to have been, as was once thought, a clear open walkway. Half-way along its length the builders preserved a small shrine, together with its altar, which seem to have pre-dated the temple. We do not know why, or what the shrine once contained. But it is a very tempting thought that the old statue of Athena might have lodged here while the temples of the Acropolis lay in ruin after the Persian invasion, and before the new Periclean building programme was under way. If that is correct (and it is only a guess), it underlines the sense in which the sculptural and architectural scheme of the Parthenon is reminding its visitors of different versions of the sacred, prompting them not merely to admire Pheidias' Athena, but to reflect on the contested nature of sacrality which it represented.

BACK TO THE FUTURE

In the long history of the city of Athens, democracy turned out to be a relatively short-lived experiment. It was restored after the end of the Great War with Sparta. The Athenian democrats, not surprisingly, took great pleasure in sending the Spartan-imposed junta packing and restoring their old political institutions. The execution of Socrates in 399 BC was one of the first, most notorious and – it must be admitted – uncharacteristic acts of the revived democracy (Socrates was not only a fearsome and irritating intellectual, he had also been closely associated with some of the most vicious anti-democrats). But, as the power politics of the Greek world were transformed by the rise of Macedon under Philip, then Alexander, Athens became increasingly outmanoeuvred, diplomatically and militarily. The final blow came in 323 when a Macedonian warlord defeated the Athenians in battle, sent in an occupying garrison and got rid of the democracy, in favour of a puppet oligarchy. Between this point and the Byzantine empire, almost a millennium later, the Athenians saw a series of nabobs, dictators, quisling governments and (eventually, from the second century BC) the new superpower of Rome in overall control of their city. Most of this control was relatively 'hands-off'; even the richest superpowers of antiquity did not have the resources to keep a particularly tight rein on their satellites. For centuries, under different regimes, Athens thrived as a university town, cultural centre and tourist magnet. There were even occasions when the forms of democracy were revived for a time, and the Romans made much of the 'freedom' they lavishly (and largely honorifically) granted to Athens in recognition of its special historic status. None the less, the radical form of popular government that had developed in the fifth century was gone for good. Through most of classical antiquity, the Parthenon, our icon of democracy, was the jewel in the crown of autocrats.

There are occasional stories, as we have already seen, of the Parthenon becoming the victim of some despicable tyrant: the thuggish Demetrios moving in with his lady friends for a short (and, no doubt, rather uncomfortable) time at the very end of the fourth century; or his rival Lakhares who is reputed to have stripped the statue of Athena to pay his soldiers. By and large, however, kings, generals and emperors preferred either to leave the building alone or to throw money at it – taking advantage of the kudos that benefaction to such a prestigious and sacred building might bring. It was almost certainly Alexander the Great, for example, who had the 14 shields blazoned across the building's eastern façade, as well as dedicating 300 suits of Persian armour to Athena. In fact these particular shields did not last long, for they were also picked off by Lakhares in the early third century. Replacements were soon fitted by some other grandee, and more shields (or perhaps metal wreaths) added down the north and south sides of the building.

In the early second century, one of the fabulously rich Attalid dynasty, based at Pergamum (in modern Turkey), went even further. The Attalids, who had come from nowhere to be big players among the competing powers of the eastern Mediterranean, looked for cultural respectability by lavishing money on Athens. Their best known memorial is the vast *stoa* (the ancient equivalent of a shopping mall) that they foisted on the Athenian city-centre; a replica now stands there, reconstructed at vast expense in the 1950s, to house the finds from American excavations. On the Acropolis they were responsible for a famous group of sculptures that picked up the themes of the Parthenon with a tableau of defeated giants, Amazons and (to reflect the Attalids' own victories) Gauls. Most eye-catchingly of all, though, they sponsored a huge memorial to one of their dynasty that practically abutted the right-hand corner of the temple's front steps. This took the form of a huge pedestal, reaching up almost to the level of the Parthenon's roof, with probably a bronze chariot on the top. For anyone standing near by, it would almost certainly have blocked the view of the adjacent metope panels, with their battles of gods and giants.

Years later, in 31 BC, when the Attalids were a thing of the past and all sensible cities were giving public backing to the brash young victor in Rome's civil war, who was shortly to become the first emperor Augustus, this monument was deftly rededicated to him. This speedy gesture was itself quickly followed, in 27 BC, by a new temple dedicated jointly to Rome and the emperor himself, erected just 25 metres from the Parthenon's front door, and on a direct axis with it. Whether this was an aggressive intrusion of Roman *Machtpolitik* into the Greek sacred landscape, or represented an elegant incorporation of new sources of Roman power into the Athenian cosmos, depends (as it always did) on your point of view.

The fate of Pheidias' cult statue through this period is something of a puzzle. If Lakhares really did remove her gold plates (and it would be hard to make sense of ancient accounts in any other way), then some kind of replacement must have been fitted – but maybe not necessarily in solid gold. Assuming no other major damage and repair, it would have been this restored version of the statue that Pausanias saw in the second century AD. It cannot have been this statue, however, that demanded house-room with our fifth-century philosopher to escape Christian destruction (pp. 54–5). For, probably sometime in the mid-third century AD, the Parthenon suffered a devastating fire that did almost as much damage to the building as would the explosion of 1687. No gold and ivory statue could possibly have survived it. Whatever the image of Athena was in the final pagan phases of the temple, it had no more than a nominal connection with Pheidias' creation.

No ancient writer mentions the fire or the subsequent

restoration. But the archaeological evidence is absolutely conclusive. The roof was destroyed, along with almost all the interior fixtures and fittings. The marble cracked, dangerously, throughout. The colonnade in the eastern chamber was ruined, as were both main doors and the second frieze. If there were any dedications still kept in store (and we have no idea how long that tradition lasted) they would certainly have been consumed by the heat and flames. The restoration that followed did not attempt to recreate all that had been lost. A roof of terracotta was fitted over the interior rooms alone; the outer colonnade was now left open to the sky (which would, at least, have had the advantage of making the outer frieze easier to see). The two tiers of columns in the eastern room were replaced by a similar structure, although this was not purpose-built. To judge from the architectural style of the replacement, the restorers must have turned to a couple of abandoned buildings of the second century BC, where they found enough columns of the right size to fit the gap. It was this re-used colonnade that featured in the Christian church and the mosque – though with a floor inserted at first-storey level, between the tiers, to make a gallery.

That much is clear. Much less certain is the date of the fire or of the repair. The best guess is that the fire was in some way connected with one of those classic invasions of northern barbarians – in this case the Heruli, who did considerable damage at Athens in 267 AD. Whether the restoration followed immediately after the fire, we do not know. But some archaeologists have suspected, on the basis of some of the material (re)used in the repair, that it may have remained more or less ruined for up to a hundred years. Whenever it took place, it was the start of a long tradition, enthusiastically carried on through the Middle Ages and later, of patching up the Parthenon with the remnants of other classical monuments from either the Acropolis itself or elsewhere in the city. The temple was to become the final resting place of some of the most notable antiquities of Athens.

This has been the theme of some of the most impressive detective work carried out by the recent restorers. They have carefully tracked down the original site and function of the blocks used by those who repaired the west doorway after the fire. Many were taken from the bases of all kinds of sculpture. These include six blocks that formed the setting for a huge group of horses and chariot dedicated by 'Pronapes' in the middle of the fifth century (the cuttings for the hooves and chariot wheels are still visible) and the base of what was almost certainly a group of bronze warriors that was seen by Pausanias not far from the temple. In fact, this offers one answer to the puzzling question of what happened to all the monuments Pausanias noted on the Acropolis. The bronze will have been melted down; the bits of marble likely as not ended up in the Parthenon itself. But the most ironic twist of all comes with some of the inscribed texts which were cannibalised to make up the new door jambs. Three of the blocks used by the repairers are none other than fragments of those fourth-century BC inventories of the treasures that had then filled the building. They make a memorable image of what had changed between the fourth centuries BC and AD; and an apt symbol of the complex history of the Parthenon.

6

MEANWHILE, BACK IN LONDON ...

FIXING A PRICE

In the spring of 1816 a galaxy of British artists were called to give evidence to the Select Committee of the House of Commons which had been appointed 'to enquire whether it be expedient that the Collection mentioned in the Earl of Elgin's petition ... should be purchased on behalf of the Public, and, if so, what Price may be reasonable to allow for the same.' Should the government buy Elgin's marbles? The Committee wanted some straight answers from the artists. Exactly how good were these sculptures? How did they rate against other masterpieces of classical art? In particular, how did they compare with those two masterpieces of the Vatican collection and the favourites of every gentleman and connoisseur – the 'most sublime' (as Winckelmann had it) Apollo Belvedere and that writhing mass of human bodies and snakes known as Laocoon? The Committee also had a hard nose for the financial side of the deal. How did the cash value of what Elgin was offering compare with that of the other great collections recently acquired for the British Museum? Sir Charles Townley's collection of Roman sculpture had been bought for £20,000; the sculpted frieze from the fifth-century temple of Apollo at Bassae in the Peloponnese (reputedly designed by the same architect as the

20. This figure from the east pediment was identified as Theseus or Hercules in the nineteenth century. More recently the god Dionysus has been thought a more likely candidate (it all rather depends what you make of the animal skin on which he is leaning – panther? lion?). Though hugely admired, the weathered surface of the sculpture and the missing hands and feet were quite unlike the image of classical perfection that early nineteenth-century taste would have expected.

Parthenon) had been knocked down for £15,000. Were Elgin's marbles worth more or less? And if more, how much more?

Most of the artists gushed with enthusiasm for the Parthenon sculptures, but were shifty when it came to the details. John Flaxman, for example, could not quite bring himself to rate the metopes and frieze higher than Laocoon. When pushed to rank the Apollo Belvedere against the figure from the east pediment then known either as the 'Hercules' or 'Theseus' (the only figure, apart from the horses, still complete with its head (*Illustration 20*)), he wriggled. They were so different that it was hard to make a judgement. The Hercules was terribly corroded; and, in any case, how could you ever compare an Apollo with a Hercules? ('The Apollo Belvidere [sic] is a divinity of a higher order than the Hercules.') So, yes, as he finally admitted, he did prefer the Apollo, even though 'I believe it is only a copy'. Others hedged their bets differently. Joseph Nollekens was happy to rate the Theseus as equal to the Apollo Belvedere, but not greater. Richard Westmacott, on the other hand, preferred the Theseus to the Apollo, but was much less certain whether it outranked Laocoon. And so on. In general, though, the Committee could only have come away with the impression that the artistic establishment thought these sculptures a tremendous catch. Even the well-known doubters cast their doubts in a relatively low key. Richard Payne Knight, who was reputed to believe the whole collection Roman (and had teased Elgin to that effect at a notorious dinner party) came out with some surprisingly mellow answers. Some of the sculptures from the pediments were, he continued to insist, added in the reign of Hadrian. Some of the metopes were very poor and some were possibly later additions; 'but the best of them I consider as the best works of high relief'. The frieze was certainly of 'high antiquity' and to be counted in 'the first class of low relief'.

The problems the artists faced in answering the Committee's questions were not simply caused by their reluctance to produce a crude rank order of works of art for a group of literal-minded Members of Parliament. All of these men had been brought up to admire such celebrity pieces as the Apollo and Laocoon, Roman sculptures (possibly, as Flaxman believed, copies or versions of earlier Greek work), discovered in Italy during the Renaissance and highly restored, to a particular image of perfection, by the best sculptors of the day. They were quite unlike these battered, incomplete fragments that were among the first sculptures from the supposed acme of classical Greece that any of these experts had ever seen – aggressively unrestored and palpably the products of a radically different aesthetic from all their old favourites. Flaxman was not just trying to avoid the question when he protested that you really could not rank the Hercules/Theseus against Apollo; it would be rather like asking a modern artist whether to rate Picasso's *Guernica* above or below Botticelli's *Primavera*.

The same issues lay behind their reluctance to attach even a relative cash value to the marbles. Here the artists squirmed even more awkwardly. Were the marbles worth more or less than the £20,000 that had been paid for Sir Charles Townley's collection? Today that question would seem hardly worth posing. Townley was one of the busiest eighteenth-century collectors, avidly buying up sculpture from dealers in Rome, most of it small scale, much of it imaginatively restored, some of it arguably fake. His collection is a priceless document of the taste and passions of an eighteenth-century connoisseur, but is now in a completely different league from the Elgin Marbles – as its present accommodation in the British Museum only too clearly indicates (not the vast shrine that houses the marbles, but a gloomy basement, little visited and usually the first gallery to be closed if there is any shortage of staff). In 1816 the comparison seemed a trickier issue. A number of the artists and other critics agreed that, from an artistic point of view, Elgin's collection was much the more valuable. But commercially, they felt, the Townley collection would fetch more. The pieces were, after all, complete, and they could be sold off individually. Nobody thought there was much chance of a collector paying any great price for some of the battered fragments that Elgin had brought home.

Lord Elgin was asking for £74,000. He himself gave evidence to the Select Committee at the very beginning of their proceedings. It was then almost 20 years since he had set off to become British ambassador to the Sultan's court; in the meantime he had gained a vast collection of sculpture (the tail end of which arrived in London only in 1815), and lost almost everything else. He had left his position in Constantinople as early as January 1803, while his agents were still hard at work on the Acropolis. From there on, every kind of disaster struck: he was imprisoned by the French on his way home in the midst of the Napoleonic War; he lost his wife, who fell for a kindly (or predatory) neighbour during his absence; he was close to bankruptcy, thanks to the cost of acquiring the marbles, paying the wages of his men, arranging storage and transport, plus the interest on his loans.

When he offered the collection to the British government, he reckoned that £74,000 would just about cover his expenses. The Select Committee would have none of it. They recommended, and parliament endorsed, the purchase of the marbles – but at the price of only £35,000. Elgin probably had no option but to accept.

The House of Commons debate which ratified the purchase by a large majority in June 1816 is striking for its sheer modernity. Though cast in the distinctive jargon of the early nineteenth century, it reveals an intense anxiety about what we would call 'sleaze' (in particular, whether Elgin had taken improper advantage of his position of ambassador to obtain his firman). Doubts were also raised about the economic constraints. Was a collection of ancient sculpture not so much a triumphalist prize to celebrate the nation's victory, but a luxury that the exchequer could ill afford in the aftermath of the extremely expensive Napoleonic War? Or, as a contemporary cartoon by George Cruikshank pictured it, was Elgin pushing his luck in attempting to sell his 'stones' to a starving John Bull, who would have preferred the £35,000 spent on bread? But beyond these familiar themes of parliamentary debate, almost every political and cultural argument that has since been used for or against the return of the marbles to Greece, or their retention in the British Museum, got a public airing. These included not only the legality of Elgin's actions and the question of where the sculpture would be best looked after, but also some of the earliest expressions of the philhellenic idea that the sculptures simply did not 'belong' in England.

One of the Members of Parliament, Mr Hugh Hammersley, reporting rumours that the Russians were about to intervene in favour of Greek independence and to establish one of their own princelings on the new Greek throne, suggested an amendment to the Select Committee's report. Why not offer Elgin £25,000 for his pains and keep the marbles in trust until 'they are demanded by the present, or any future, possessors of the city of Athens'? The response to this amendment was the ridicule that Hammersley must have expected. Sending the marbles back to those who had wilfully damaged them would have been bad enough; but, as the next speaker huffed and puffed, the suggestion that the British should keep them in trust for the Russians was 'one of the most absurd ever heard in the House'. For us it is a neat reminder that proposals to repatriate the marbles began even before Parliament had made its final decision to buy them for the nation. Their presence in Britain has never been uncontested or uncontroversial.

MUSEUM OBJECTS

In 1817 the Elgin Marbles were put on view to the public in a temporary room hurriedly erected at the old British Museum in Montagu House. Here the sculptures from the Parthenon jostled with many of the other antiquities that had ended up, thanks to his agents, in Elgin's packing cases: not just the famous caryatid from the porch of the Erechtheion, but some bits and pieces from Mycenae, a whole variety of architectural fragments, some plaster casts of other material not removed from Greece, as well as a notable statue of the god Dionysus from a monument on the Acropolis slopes. In fact, as contemporary paintings show, pride of place in the new room went to the Dionysus, who stood in the apse at one end, supported by a column capital from the Parthenon. On either side were two reclining male figures, one from the west and one (Theseus/Hercules) from the east pediment, and leading up to this ensemble was a long gallery, lined with the metopes, frieze and the various other casts and fragments. No attempt was made to recapture the original placement of the sculpture, nor to separate what belonged to the Parthenon from the rest. It was a 'picturesque' arrangement, whose main purpose was to provide the most congenial atmosphere for artists to draw. Many of the most famous pieces were fixed on to swivelling bases, so that they could be moved to catch the best light (*Illustration 21*).

There is a world of difference between this and the spotless, austere regime in place today, in the custom-built gallery financed by Joseph Duveen in the 1930s (though not regularly open to the public until 1962). In the intervening years, different arrangements of the marbles were proposed and sometimes bitterly debated by the museum curators. And a whole series of new styles of display was attempted and contested – each one reflecting not just changing fashion, but changing understanding of the objects themselves and of the museum's role in presenting and interpreting them. The debates were so intense and the process of decision-making so slow that the marbles seem to have spent many years of the nineteenth century lying around the museum 'in the course of rearrangement'. Understandably perhaps – since, underneath some of the apparently petty squabbles, crucial questions were at stake. Were the Elgin Marbles to be seen as 'great art'? Or as part of the grand historical development of world culture that the British Museum documented? And what difference did that make to their style of display?

Should the museum be stressing the original architectural context in which the sculptures were first displayed? Should it be teaching its visitors about the Parthenon as a whole, not just displaying the masterpieces that once decorated it? Or was the aesthetic power of the sculptures alone to be the leading principle?

There were no easy answers. For much of the nineteenth century it might look as if the trend was towards an increasingly archaeological and didactic style of display. From the moment that the sculptures were moved into their first 'permanent' gallery in 1832 in Robert Smirke's new museum building, the various elements of the Parthenon itself were more coherently arranged. The figures from the pediment, for example, were placed together on plinths in more or less their 'correct' order. By the 1850s some of the museum staff were arguing that they should be shown inside a frame that copied the distinctive shape of the pediment, or even fixed high up so that they could be seen 'correctly' from below. A famous anecdote about a learned German visitor who had been forced to lie down on the floor to capture the right angle of vision was wheeled out in support of this kind of radical change. Meanwhile models of the Parthenon, as ruin and as reconstructed, were introduced into the gallery. And, in order to make it easier to understand the whole of the sculptural scheme, plaster casts of what remained in Athens were systematically incorporated into the display. This was partly a question of inserting casts of sections of the frieze that were needed to complete the narrative. But it could also mean attaching the cast of a missing foot or arm directly on to the ancient marble. For us, the single most surprising feature of this early display of the Parthenon

21. The Elgin Marbles in their first temporary accommodation in the British
Museum, surrounded by an admiring throng of staff from the museum and
its library, plus the artist Benjamin West (seated centre left), the President of
the Royal Academy. The centrepiece sculpture in the apse is a statue of
Dionysus (not from the Parthenon itself). This is flanked on the right by
Theseus/Hercules (*Illustration 20*) and the horse of the moon (*Illustration
16*); on the left by a figure of a 'river god' (?) from the west pediment.

22. The architect's scheme for the Duveen Gallery. Predictably enough, Duveen called the tune with the choice of architect (an American, J. Russell Pope). The plans went through various stages before the scheme shown here was approved. The museum authorities were worried that the sculpture appeared too remote from the visitor and that it was dominated by the gallery's architecture.

sculpture is the prominence it gave to plaster copies; about 60 per cent of the frieze on show was original, about 40 per cent plaster cast.

But this didactic imperative never entirely won out. It was always held in check by the competing pressure to display the marbles as 'great art'. So, for example, no sooner had the helpful model of the reconstructed Parthenon been introduced into the gallery than it was hastily removed to the basement. It simply did not come up to the required aesthetic standard; or, as the keeper of the day put it, 'the coarseness of its execution and the restored portions [are] quite unworthy of the original remains'. And in the 1850s there was a serious proposal that the Parthenon sculptures (and other major sculpture in the British Museum) should be transferred to a new National Gallery, to be displayed side by side with masterpieces of painting. One of those who were called in to advise and strongly opposed any such mixture of media was the elderly Leo von Klenze, gallery designer for Ludwig of Bavaria and renowned architect, whom we last met as mastermind of the Acropolis pageant in 1834.

The proposal failed. But some 70 years later, in 1928, an official report on the display of the Parthenon sculpture was happy to start from the assumption that the marbles were 'primarily works of art', and that 'their present educational use' is 'by comparison, accidental and trivial'. These were the carefully chosen words of a highbrow committee (consisting of three heavyweight classical archaeologists) who went on to recommend a crucial change in the layout of the material in the museum. No longer were the sculptures to be supplemented with plaster casts. 'The juxtaposition', they wrote, 'of marble and plaster is bound to be inharmonious'; the originals, fragmentary as they were, ought to be viewed and admired without any such distraction. The recently retired Keeper of Antiquities instantly saw the point. It was a victory for the transcendent quality of original masterpieces over completeness, context and history; it was a victory for the Parthenon as sculpture over the Parthenon as building. It implied, he observed (not entirely accurately, given the century of fierce debates), 'a reversal of the policy that has been pursued for about a hundred years'.

The current display in the Duveen Gallery represents a predictably awkward compromise between these two different imperatives (*Illustration 22*). The sheer vastness of the gallery space signals the cultural and artistic importance of the works of art housed within it; no visitor could fail to see that they were supposed to *admire*. Context, history and casts (now including a hands-on display for the blind) are part of the show, but firmly relegated to two side-rooms next to the main entrance; they are not to encroach on the original marbles. The layout of the gallery does indeed gesture towards the architectural coherence of the monument itself: the pediments stand at each end of the room; the frieze runs around the central space (albeit turned 'inside out', to face inwards rather than outwards, as it did in its original position). But the real trick of the arrangement is to present the Elgin Marbles as if they were a complete set. Casual observers would never guess that a substantial section of the frieze still remained in Athens. And, if the architect's original plans had been followed, they would hardly have noticed that much of the east pediment was missing either. It was only the purists among the museum staff who insisted on leaving a tell-tale gap on the plinths to mark where the key central figures had been lost. Overall the effect (and the intention) of the gallery design is to efface what remains in Athens. If the earlier regimes of display repeatedly and explicitly referred the viewer to the monument in Greece and its surviving sculpture, the Duveen effect is to squeeze that memory out. The Elgin Marbles are here meant to stand for the Parthenon itself.

SURFACE TENSION

The interventions of Joseph Duveen – an immensely rich and not entirely scrupulous art dealer – have become notorious in the history of the Parthenon sculptures. Anxious for that combination of immortality and respectability that only lavish public benefactions can buy, he ploughed money into various major projects in London galleries as well as providing new accommodation for the Elgin Marbles. Progress at the British Museum was much slower than he had hoped. Although the project had been dreamt up and the funding promised in the late 1920s, it was not until 1936 that the building land had been acquired and work started on what was to become the Duveen Gallery. By that stage Duveen was terminally ill (he died in 1939) and, one would guess, more than usually demanding and difficult to deal with. Somehow or other (most likely through tiresome persistence) he and his agents managed to get hold of keys to the relevant museum galleries and to enjoy virtually free access to the Parthenon sculptures which were being prepared for their new installation. They also seem to have taken direct control of some of the museum's assistants and technicians.

Or so at least the director concluded, after he had wandered through the workshops in the museum basement one Sunday night in September 1938 and noticed on a bench a group from the east pediment, the Sun and his horses; it was obviously 'in process of cleaning'. As the official report on the incident continues, 'he observed a number of copper tools and a piece of coarse carborundum, and from the appearance of the sculptures he at once saw that the tools had been used on the sculptures'. The next day two other figures from the pediment, including the famous horse of the Moon, were found to be undergoing similar treatment elsewhere in the museum. 'The Director ordered all further cleaning operations to be stopped and instituted an inquiry into what had occurred.'

The bare outline is clear enough. Duveen wanted the works of art in his new gallery to look the part: pure, white and *classical*. The Elgin Marbles were not only dirty (a combination of London smog and the museum's heating system), they were also covered in various places with an orange-brown 'patina' or 'coating'. Duveen's agents asked the museum's workmen to give them a good clean, while the curators for whatever reason turned a blind eye, over a period of more than a year. Copper tools and carborundum were, obviously, inappropriate instruments to use on the sculpture – even though, it is important to remember, ancient marble used often to be cleaned much more abrasively than we would expect today (Michelangelo's David was scrubbed with wire-wool in the nineteenth century and, as late as the 1950s, the sculptures of the Theseum were given a rough treatment similar to Duveen's by an American team working in Athens). The internal investigation prompted a good deal of buck-passing and self-interested exculpation, but heads did, discreetly, roll and 'remedial measures' (the phrase alone makes you shudder) were taken on the marbles.

It was not, however, kept out of the press, where the usual range of up-market hacks and professional letter-writers pondered on quite how much of the 'patina' had been lost and from where. The sculptor Jacob Epstein thundered characteristically: 'Why a cleaner and six hefty men should be allowed for fifteen months to tamper with the Elgin Marbles … passes the comprehension of a sculptor'. The travel writer Robert Byron, no relation to the poet despite the name (which none the less stood him in very good stead in Greece), lost no opportunity to swipe at Elgin and to point out that 'for a hundred years the London atmosphere has been encrusting those once sun-kissed figures with a sheath of corrosive soot'. Others, self-styled philistines, wondered what all the fuss was about. As the *Star* reported in March 1939, 'somebody … started giving these B.M. marbles a wash and brush up, thus jeopardising, in the opinion of some, the exquisite patina – the accumulation of grime caused by long exposure to atmosphere. Like mouldy bits of gorgonzola, this patina is much admired by artistic epicures.' Inevitably questions were asked in Parliament, but by the summer of 1939 most people had more important things on their minds. As the marbles were sandbagged and later carted off to safe keeping, divided between the museum basement and Aldwych underground station, the issues of the 'cleaning' were largely forgotten; as they were also when the sculptures were eventually returned to permanent display in the 'new' Duveen Gallery in 1962.

This story, however, has an unexpected sequel. In the late 1990s Duveen's cleaning was unearthed and re-investigated by a distinguished scholar working on the history of Elgin's collection. By the time it had reached the press, the whole affair was treated not merely as a salutary lesson in the dangers that millionaire benefactors can bring to a museum and its contents (though that is probably the story's most significant moral). It turned from a cock-up into a major conspiracy, a dreadful secret of the British Museum that had been revealed, 60 years later, for the very first time. No one, of course, cared to remember the pages of newspaper coverage and parliamentary questions of the 1930s. To its credit (even if some felt that the gesture came a little too late for comfort), the British Museum responded by holding an international conference in 1999 to try to get to the bottom of the events of 1938. Members of the Greek archaeological service came to debate the issues with scholars from Britain, Germany and the United States, in the presence of several hundred neutral and not-so-neutral experts and observers. Top of the agenda were two questions. What exactly was the orange-brown coating on the Parthenon marbles, both in Athens and London? And what damage was done under Duveen's auspices?

The surfaces of the Elgin Marbles are the product of more than two millennia of treatment, cleaning, assault, weathering and decay. It is now next to impossible to reconstruct how the marble looked when the building was first built. The sculptures were presumably painted (but how much and how garishly remains an open question); they would also have featured various attachments – metal fittings for the horses' harnesses on the frieze and a variety of accessories, from metal belts to weaponry, for the divine and human figures. But all trace of the original surface is long lost. Even if anything had survived to the beginning of the nineteenth century (which is itself extremely unlikely), there is no chance that the pristine surface could have withstood whatever 'wash and brush-up' Elgin's men administered, the perils of their journey to England (which for one consignment included a short time at the bottom of the sea) and the effects of taking moulds for plaster casts directly from the marble. Meanwhile in Greece wear and tear, combined with the pollution and acid rain, would have been even more corrosive for any sculptures left on the monument itself (*Illustration 23*).

The coating which does survive is certainly not the original surface as it would have appeared to visitors in the fifth century BC. (The Periclean Parthenon was *not* orange-brown.) But it *is*, equally certainly, ancient, for it has itself been weathered in exposed parts and various ancient repairs, alterations and adjustments to the sculptures have actually cut through it. So what is it? The old idea was that it was staining caused by iron oxide leaching out of the marble over time. But, as was agreed at the conference, that now seems most improbable. The coating is much more likely to be the product of some kind of 'wash' applied to the marble when it was first built, either as a base for the application of paint, or as a treatment intended to reduce the glare of the natural stone. Whatever the exact composition of this wash, in time, exposed to the open air, it turned into this distinctively coloured patina. As such it has a certain scientific interest, but it is not the 'original surface' in any meaningful sense of the term. At Duveen's direct or indirect behest, along with a good deal of grime, some of this coating was removed from the sculptures. About 60 per cent of the surface of the metopes was cleaned, considerably less of the frieze and pediments (though, of course, the 'coating' had not survived on all the parts that were cleaned). Quite how much damage was done depends on your point of view. No one would now advocate such a cleaning operation, certainly not driven by a wealthy and wilful 'benefactor'. But it is significant that, until the story was publicised again in the 1990s, most visitors to the British Museum (even professional archaeologists) noticed nothing wrong; such damage as there was, was not obvious.

You could never guess from these sober, careful and altogether unsurprising conclusions quite how angry, emotional and even, at one point, almost violent the conference in 1999 was. Here was an academic discussion of an ill-judged cleaning programme of some fifth-century BC marble sculpture; the events had all happened more than 60 years before and none of the major players were still alive. Yet the conference attracted front-page press reports across Europe and widespread television coverage in Greece. Several of the participants and commentators chose to present the issues in terms that would be rhetorically more appropriate for human victims of outrage than for lumps of stone; there was talk, for example, of Duveen's futile attempts to 'beautify' the marbles, which really amounted to 'torture' or 'atrocity'. The final session nearly came to blows. Why? Why such a gap between the intrinsic importance of the case and the moral fervour and intensity with which it was debated?

A MONUMENT WORTH THE FIGHT?

A lot of issues were in play. To some the British Museum seemed to be on the defensive. There was a whiff of conspiracy and cover-up. Those who believed that they had

23. The marbles left in Athens have not survived unscathed. On the left is a cast of part of the west frieze taken from a mould made by Lord Elgin's agents. On the right, a cast made from a mould of 1872 shows the damage and deterioration of some seventy years – even before the effects of serious air pollution.

unearthed a hidden scandal at the heart of one of the country's most elite institutions were committed to getting the whole affair out of proportion. But more important was the 200-year-old question of where the Elgin Marbles rightly belonged. From the early nineteenth century the issue of 'stewardship' has always been central to these debates. Elgin's actions have been, and still are, regularly defended by the simple claim that the marbles have been safer in England. Left on the Acropolis, so the argument has always gone, they would have found their way into Turkish cement or been used as target practice by bored soldiers, cooped up on the hill during the War of Independence; at least in Britain they were properly looked after. Duveen's actions opened a vulnerable chink in that otherwise strong position. Never mind the condition of the sculptures left on the Parthenon itself, the Greeks and other supporters of the return of the marbles were bound to play Duveen's folly for all it was worth. Two centuries of British self-satisfaction had it coming.

The emotional intensity of the conference was driven by one of the most enduring cultural controversies in the modern world. Should the Elgin Marbles be returned to Greece? This issue has become so much part of British popular culture that, over the last decade or so, it has provided the backdrop to novels and even the theme of some virtuoso internet games. Web surfers who have visited electroasylum.com/elgin have been able to try their hand at the ingenious Elgin Marbles Game, where punters can throw electronic marbles (the round glass variety) at the seventh Earl. Depending on where you hit poor Elgin, he shudders disquietingly or (if you are right on target) disintegrates into a macromedia display of flashing red lights. In the world of recent thrillers, Reg Gadney's *Strange Police* wove a complex story of blackmail, vendetta and adultery around a Greek conspiracy to steal the marbles from the British Museum. Though armed with an impressive array of freightwagons, Chinooks and a conveniently spare Boeing, the thieves fail to prise out a single sculpture; and one of them ends up very dead on the floor of the Duveen Gallery, having suffered a nasty fall from the roof.

Among such more or less engaging fantasies, the arguments themselves have sometimes failed to match our expectations. In the recent rounds of the controversy there have certainly been some dishonourable incidents. The heat-of-the-moment claim by one director of the British Museum that anyone who wanted to return the marbles to Greece was a 'cultural fascist' ('It's like burning books. That's what Hitler did') must mark, by some wide margin, the lowest point. But the self-righteousness of some of the British Left (who have found a comfortably armchair-radical cause in this particular brand of philhellenism) can be pretty hard to stomach too. Not to mention the vulgar nationalism of some of the Greek arguments, with their optimistic assurance that the inhabitants of modern Greece are the spiritual, if not literal, heirs of Pericles and his friends.

This was a claim that, inevitably, hovered at the edge of the latest round of British parliamentary discussions of the whole question of the Elgin Marbles. In summer 2000, in what seemed rather like a belated sequel to the proceedings of 1816, the Select Committee for Culture, Media and Sport, investigating the illicit trade of cultural property, considered the case of the British Museum and the Parthenon sculptures. As before, distinguished witnesses were called. But not this time artists, sculptors and critics. It was a mark of the changed cultural and political climate that the cross-questioning was directed to three representatives of the British Museum and three representatives sent by the Greek government. If the quality of the sculpture was not on this occasion in debate (in fact one wonders how many of these expert witnesses would have been able to offer any comparison between Laocoon and the so-called 'Theseus'), several other issues were the same – notably the old chestnuts of good care and legal ownership. Displaying a rather weaker grip on the basic facts than one might have hoped, one of the Members of Parliament asked the spokesmen of the British Museum, '... you say legally we hold them. Obviously, you can prove that. By what means? Is there a document? We are told there is a piece of paper somewhere. Is there such a thing?'

As Flaxman and his colleagues discovered in 1816, appearing as a witness before a parliamentary select committee can be a daunting game. In summer 2000, the representatives of the Museum stood their ground on issues of ownership calmly, refused to be drawn on comparisons between the marbles and the latest case of a tug-of-love child, and occasionally overplayed their hand. When asked, for example, about the problem of an individual piece of sculpture divided between Greece and England ('head ... here and a body and tail in Athens'), one of them suggested that the best solution was that all the pieces come to London: 'because we feel we have a brief to communicate to a very substantial world audience and can do it better than anyone else'. No wonder 'anyone else' might have felt insulted.

On the other side, George Papandreou, the shrewd Greek minister, played his hand with skill. He refused to be drawn on the legality of Elgin's actions or on questions of 'ownership'. 'Who owns the sculptures', he claimed, 'is unimportant'; what matters is where they are and how 'we write their history for the future'. If the marbles made their 'homecoming' for the Olympic Games in 2004, taking pride of place in the (as yet unbuilt) new Acropolis Museum, then all kinds of new Anglo-Hellenic partnerships were in prospect, not to mention 'a permanent spot of warmth and gratitude of the Greek people throughout the world'. It was a well-judged performance. His colleague, however, the elderly Jules Dassin, was more of a liability. Dassin had become an obligatory presence on such delegations in his role as widower of Melina Mercouri, the actress and Greek Minister of Culture who still remains the symbol of the campaign for the marbles' return (her portrait is, significantly enough, now immortalised in the platform decoration of the Acropolis subway station in Athens). A film director, he was the closest to an artist that this select committee saw ('certainly one of the great film directors – I will not say the greatest film director', as Gerald Kaufman, the committee chair, introduced him, with characteristic frankness). As a witness before a parliamentary inquiry, he was out of his depth. 'We are here all sweetness and light to talk about reconciliation,' he oozed at one point. At another he quoted his wife's view that Greek sculpture in a European museum was in general 'very box office'. Not surprisingly perhaps, the committee ended up making no specific recommendations about the future of the marbles at all. Whether the discussions, for all their polite noises about 'mutual understanding', had any impact on this sharply polarised dispute is a moot point.

Bad arguments, like good ones, come and go. The controversy, as a whole, continues because it reflects a real and important conflict about the role of cultural heritage, the responsibility for the classical past and the function of symbolic monuments. Like it or not, the case on both sides is powerful; otherwise the dilemma would have been resolved long since. No one could deny the coherence and appeal of having all the sculpture from the Parthenon in one place. But it is equally clear that after 200 years the Elgin Marbles have a history that roots them in the British Museum as well as in Athens; and that history cannot simply be unwritten by a well-meaning gesture of 'restitution'. No one could deny that a special connection has developed between the Parthenon and the Greek nation. But, at the same time, classical culture and its symbols have for centuries transcended national boundaries. As the then British Minister for the Arts said, albeit slightly ponderously, in *his* evidence to the 2000 Select Committee: ' I understand the emotional importance … to the Greek people of this case. I would also say with respect that we too in this country are heirs to the classical tradition. I would say that the diffusion of the classical culture of ideas, values and of physical relics and monuments over two millennia, has contributed in profoundly important ways to the history that has led to the emergence of the world that we have. It seems to me unthinkable that we should wish to reverse that process.'

But the bottom line, despite the brave claims of George Papandreou, is always the issue of ownership. To whom does the Parthenon belong? Masterpieces in other media can escape this impasse. Shakespeare, after all, can belong to, and be performed by, everyone in the world, as well as having a special link with Stratford-upon-Avon. The sense in which he 'belongs' to Stratford does not deprive anyone else of their own engagement with the bard and his work. The same would be true of Mozart and Vienna. Buildings are different. And the Parthenon raises that difference in an acute form. The debate that surrounds the Elgin Marbles forces us to face the unanswerable question of who can, and should, own the monument. Does it count as the possession of all those who would love to see themselves as the inheritors of the values of fifth-century Athens? Or those whose capital city it dominates? Can a single monument act as a symbol both of nationhood and of world culture?

Inevitably, then, the Parthenon and its sculpture have come to stand for deracination, dismemberment, desire and loss. Freud was more astute than we first imagined when he wondered if the Parthenon really did exist at all, in Athens or anywhere else for that matter. For the Parthenon is always 'somewhere else'. If not entirely absent, it is never wholly present. Like Byron and his followers we may weep at the thought. But it is partly that sense of loss, absence and desire that now gives the monument its cultural power and urgency. Paradoxically, its status as international icon can hardly be disentangled from its diaspora that so many of us lament. Not just from Athens to London, but from Uppsala to Palermo, Nashville to Heidelberg, the Parthenon is literally a wonder of the world.

MAKING A VISIT?

Until 2010, or thereabouts, the pleasure of a visit to the *Parthenon* itself will be limited to the outside of the building. The inside will be glimpsed only through an impressive, but intrusive, array of scaffolding and engineering tackle. Even the colonnade and steps are firmly off-limits until the current restoration programme (which is to include a section of the Christian church, as well as the fifth-century BC temple) is complete. Then it is hoped to allow some public access again, probably along a series of designated walkways. The days of wandering freely around the Parthenon, indeed around the Acropolis as a whole, are almost certainly gone for good.

Many of the substantial pieces of sculpture left on or around the Parthenon by Lord Elgin and others are now on display in the *Acropolis Museum*, discreetly tucked away to the east of the Parthenon itself. But most of its space is devoted to the finds from the nineteenth-century excavations on the Acropolis, which turned up vivid evidence for the pre-classical (mostly sixth-century BC) period of the site (pp. 103–5). This includes a magnificent collection of female statues (Goddesses? Human worshippers? We cannot usually be sure), as well as the sculpture that once decorated the pediments of early temples and other buildings on the Acropolis.

But you will look in vain for any trace of the later history of the site here. In keeping with the priorities of the excavators whose finds now fill it, this is emphatically a museum of the fifth century BC and its antecedents.

The Acropolis Museum is currently suffering the museological equivalent of planning blight. Beyond its rather old-fashioned labels (and some regulation tirades against Lord Elgin), there is very little information offered to help make sense of the material on display. The series of pedimental sculptures, in particular, will baffle even the most expert visitor; and the truth is (despite the confident reconstructions shown here) we still do not know for certain exactly which pieces go with which, or in some cases which buildings they decorated. The blight is caused by the promise of a brand *new museum* to house all this material, plus the Elgin Marbles, if and when they are returned to Greece. After a troubled planning history and the last-minute cancellation of one project for the new building, this museum, on a site just to the south of the Acropolis, is now supposed to be up and running in time for the Olympic Games of 2004 (with building work starting only in the spring of 2002). It is a state-of-the-art design by New York architect Bernard Tschumi, and will feature a great glass Parthenon Hall with direct views of the temple some 300 metres away. Here the intention is to arrange the sculpture as it originally stood on the monument itself. If the Elgin Marbles are not returned, the hall will remain largely empty – a powerful symbol (or one that is rather too obviously contrived, depending on your point of view) of the feelings of absence and loss that we have seen regularly evoked by the Parthenon and its sculpture.

Other museums in Athens offer some glimpse of the later

history of Parthenon. The *Benaki Museum* (Ave Vas. Sofias) features some vivid images of the Acropolis in the eighteenth and nineteenth centuries, including some eye-witness paintings of Elgin's agents at work. It also has an excellent display on the Greek War of Independence and the role in it of European philhellenes such as Byron (who were neither so numerous nor significant as their self-advertisements tend to suggest). The *Museum of the City of Athens* (Klafmonas Sq.) is housed in the first temporary palace of young King Otto, before he moved to the pile in Syntagma Square. Its displays capture the style of Athens (including its ancient monuments) in the early years of Otto's reign. In the *Byzantine Museum* (Ave Vas. Sofias), among a baffling display of medieval carved masonry whose original location is utterly lost, there are one or two pieces known to have come from the Christian Parthenon.

LONDON

In the British Museum the Parthenon sculptures are displayed in the frankly cavernous Duveen Gallery (pp. 167–8). Despite a wealth of information panels, books, videos and audio-guides, the challenge for any visitor is to recapture any sense of how the sculpture, and in particular the frieze, was arranged on the building itself. To understand the frieze, there are two key points to remember. First, it is displayed in the gallery 'inside out'; that is, what originally decorated the outside of the Parthenon's chamber walls is here shown running round the inside of the room. Second, the display has been designed to disguise the fact that large sections of the frieze are in Athens. In order to bring this off, it must effectively dismantle the original shape and layout of the sculpture, as it was on the temple. So, for example, the *peplos* scene (*Illustration 14*), which was originally in the centre of the short east end, is now slightly off-centre on one of the long sides of the room. Most visitors will find themselves defeated by the spatial gymnastics required to reconstruct the original arrangement, including the missing parts, in any detail. The simplest plan is to orientate a visit around the *peplos* scene (clearly visible almost opposite the door as you enter) and to remember that almost nothing of the frieze at the west end was brought to London. The only two slabs from this part of the frieze are immediately on your right as you come in (where the north-west angle of the building is clearly marked). Alternatively, just enjoy it.

The pediments and metope panels do not present such difficulties. The east pediment is to the right, the west to the left, as you enter the gallery. In both cases the effect of the display is to make them look much more complete than they really are; you certainly could not fit the lost birth of Athena and its attendant figures into the gap left here in the centre of the east pediment. The metopes are now divided between the two ends of the gallery but, in fact, they all come from the south side of the building.

How much damage was actually done to these sculptures in the 1930s (pp. 168–73)? Although the conference in 1999 reached some broad agreement about what happened under the auspices of Duveen and about the overall state of the damage, there remains intense disagreement about the condition of many individual pieces. But some of them provide a clear and relatively uncontroversial introduction to the whole question:

❀ For the best, uninterrupted and close-up view of the orange-brown 'coating' that was so much at issue, look at the fragments in the showcases in the left-hand information room, before you enter the main gallery (Duveen was not the slightest bit concerned with these 'minor' pieces). You should then be able to spot it at various places on the pediments, frieze and metopes.

❀ For a lesson in the complexity of the history of the marble surfaces, try south metope XXVII (*Illustration 18*) at the right-hand end of the gallery. This metope was hardly touched by the 1930s cleaning, though a little coating on the Greek's cloak may have been removed. The apparent drips on the marble are caused by natural weathering, where ridges of harder stone are exposed as the softer stone erodes. There is also a clear 'weather line' on the Greek's leg: the outer surfaces are obviously weathered, but where it was protected (on the inner sides and between his thighs) the surface retains its smooth, polished appearance.

❀ For a clear indication of the visible effects of the cleaning, the figure of the goddess Hebe (?) (also known as 'figure G') on the east pediment provides the best example. In good light there is an obvious 'tide-mark' near the top of her thigh: below is cleaned, above is not. This is where the workmen abruptly stopped when the museum authorities discovered what was going on. Compare also the back of the head of the horse of the Moon with its front (*Illustration 17*). The back has been cleaned, the front has not. To judge from early photographs, there was only a little surviving coating to be removed, but the surface was made much smoother (a 'skinned' appearance, as the museum's own enquiry in 1938 put it).

🐚 For trace of 'original' paint, go to the back of figure E (perhaps the goddess Demeter or Persephone) on the east pediment. On the base (just below the rectangular cutting) is an obvious brush stroke – known affectionately in the museum as 'the brush stroke of Pheidias'. Although the effects of two and a half millennia have made this a rather dark daub, it was probably originally a light colour, and a test stroke by a workman, trying out his paint where it would not be noticed. If you look carefully you will see how the coating still visible here goes over the paint (and is therefore later than it). But you can see too that the coating itself has weathered, suggesting that it is an ancient, if not an 'original', element on the monument.

The two information rooms on either side of the main entrance contain important material that many visitors miss. On the right-hand side is a cast of the west frieze, made from moulds taken by Elgin's agents. Comparison with the original sculpture in Athens provides clear evidence of the environmental damage done over the last 200 years (*Illustration 23*). In the left-hand room is a third-century AD Roman version of the shield of the great statue of Athena and one of our main sources of information on its design. There is also further vivid evidence of damage to the sculpture, this time under Turkish rule. A slab of the north frieze survived pretty well intact up to the mid-eighteenth century, and was drawn complete by Stuart and Revett. All Elgin's agents could find was the small fragment on display here (together with a copy of Stuart and Revett's drawing). Presumably the rest of the slab had been smashed, re-used in building or ground into cement.

FURTHER READING

GENERAL AND INTRODUCTORY

P. Tournikiotis (ed.), *The Parthenon and its Impact in Modern Times* (Athens, 1994) is a lavishly illustrated collection of essays on the history and influence of the monument from the classical world to the present day. Much the same territory is covered in P. Green, *The Parthenon* (New York, 1973) – out-of-print, but well worth getting hold of. The wider context of the Acropolis as a whole is the theme of J. Hurwit, *The Athenian Acropolis: history, mythology, and archaeology from the neolithic era to the present* (Cambridge, 1999).

An excellent introduction to many aspects of the classical Greek history that forms the background to the building of the Parthenon is R. Osborne (ed.), *Classical Greece: 500–323 BC* (Oxford, 2000); so too is P. Cartledge (ed.) *The Cambridge Illustrated History of Ancient Greece* (Cambridge, 1998). For the art and architecture of the period, try R. Osborne, *Archaic and Classical Greek Art* (Oxford, 1998) and M. Beard and J. Henderson, *Classical Art: from Greece to Rome* (Oxford, 2001). M. Beard and J. Henderson, *Classics: a very short introduction* (Oxford, 1995) is exactly what it claims to be – a beginner's guide to the study of classical culture, its archaeology, literature and history.

CHAPTER I

Freud's reaction to the Parthenon is recorded in his 'A displacement of memory on the Acropolis', in *The Standard Edition of the Complete Psychological Works of Sigmund Freud*, vol. 22 (London, 1964). Conflicting modern reactions to the Parthenon and what it symbolises (including – carefully anonymised – the story of William Golding) are explored by P. Green, 'The shadow of the Parthenon', in his collection, *The Shadow of the Parthenon: studies in ancient history and literature* (London, 1972). J. P. Mahaffy's *Rambles in Greece* (3rd edn., London, 1887) is a wonderful glimpse of Anglo-Irish engagement with Greece and its monuments in the late nineteenth century. His pupil Oscar Wilde's first reaction to the Parthenon is buried in Julia C. Fletcher (writing as George Fleming), *Mirage* (Boston, 1878). Walker Percy's boredom is described in his *Lost in the Cosmos: the last self-help book* (London, 1984), while Evelyn Waugh came up with 'Stilton' in *Labels: a Mediterranean journal* (London, 1930). The Nashville Parthenon is the subject of W. R. Creighton and L. R. Johnson, *The Parthenon in Nashville: pearl of the Tennessee Centennial Exposition* (Tennessee, 1989). Byron's major attacks on Elgin are in *Childe Harold's Pilgrimage* (Canto II) and *The Curse of Minerva*. His stay in Athens is described by B. Eisler, *Byron: child of passion, fool of fame* (London, 1999). The broader context of these reactions to Greece are explored by D. Roessel, *In Byron's Shadow: modern Greece in the English and American imagination* (Oxford, 2002). For Elgin on the Acropolis, see below, Chapter 4. Reactions to the Elgin Marbles in London are well documented in W. St Clair, *Lord Elgin and the Marbles: the controversial history of the Parthenon sculptures* (3rd edn., Oxford,

1998) and in B. F. Cook, *The Elgin Marbles* (2nd edn., London, 1997). The trade in plaster casts is the subject of I. Jenkins's article, 'Acquisition and supply of casts of the Parthenon sculptures by the British Museum, 1835–1939', in the *Annual of the British School at Athens* 85 (1990).

CHAPTER 2

Translations of the relevant sections of Pausanias (*Guide to Greece*, Book 1), Plutarch (*Life of Pericles*) and Thucydides (*History*; the 'Funeral Speech' starts at Book 2, chapter 34) are available in the Penguin Classics series. Pausanias' *Guide* is discussed from various angles, ancient and modern, in S. E. Alcock, J. F. Cherry and J. Elsner (eds), *Pausanias: travel and memory in Roman Greece* (New York, 2001). Part of the building accounts are translated in C. W. Fornara, *Translated Documents of Greece and Rome: archaic times to the end of the Peloponnesian War* (2nd edn., Cambridge, 1983) no 120; they are discussed by A. Burford, 'The builders of the Parthenon', in G. T. W. Hooker (ed.), *Parthenos and Parthenon* (supplement to *Greece and Rome* 10, 1963).

A trenchant discussion of the pros and cons of the fifth-century BC Athenian empire is offered by M. I. Finley, 'The Athenian empire: a balance sheet', in his *Economy and Society in Ancient Greece* (London, 1981). The gold and ivory statue of Athena is minutely dissected by K. D. S. Lapatin, *Chryselephantine Statuary in the Ancient Mediterranean World* (Oxford, 2001). The processes of quarrying and transportation are enlivened by M. Korres, *From Pentelicon to the Parthenon* (Athens, 1995). For the painting of the Parthenon, see below, Chapter 6; for the frieze, Chapter 5. The idea of a Greek temple is discussed by L. Bruit Zaidmann and P. Schmitt Pantel in *Religion in the Ancient Greek City* (Cambridge, 1992). L. Kallet considers issues of finance and bookkeeping in 'Accounting for culture in fifth-century Athens', in D. Boedeker and K. Raaflaub (eds), *Democracy. Empire, and the Arts in Fifth-Century Athens* (Cambridge, Mass., 1998).

CHAPTER 3

Selected passages from Michael Choniates, Cyriac of Ancona, Evliya Celebi and Anna Åkerhjelm are translated (sometimes rather freely) in K. Andrews, *Athens Alive* (Athens, 1979). Michael is discussed by K. M. Setton, 'Athens in the later twelfth century', in his *Athens in the Middle Ages* (London, 1975); the full text of his work is available only in Greek (ed. S. Lambros, 1879–80). Niccolò is briefly discussed (with the original Latin text) in J. M. Paton, *Medieval and Renaissance Visitors to Greek Lands* (Princeton, 1951). C. Mitchell scrutinises Cyriac in 'Ciriaco d'Ancona: fifteenth-century drawings and descriptions of the Parthenon', in V. J. Bruno, *The Parthenon* (New York, 1974). Evliya's sections on Athens have never been fully translated into English, though there are two modern Greek versions, by K. I. Biris (1959) and N. Cheiladakis (1991). The account of J. Spon and G. Wheler was published in English by Wheler as *A Journey into Greece in the Company of Dr Spon of Lyons* (London, 1682). 'Carrey's' drawings are published and discussed in T. Bowie and D. Thimme, *The Carrey Drawings of the Parthenon Sculptures* (Bloomington, Ind., 1971). An eye-witness account of the bombardment of 1687, by Cristoforo Ivanovich, is translated in Bruno, *The Parthenon*.

[194]

CHAPTER 4

The main eighteenth- and nineteenth-century travellers' accounts referred to in this chapter are: R. Chandler, *Travels in Greece* (Oxford, 1776); E. Dodwell, *A Classical and Topographical Tour through Greece* (London, 1819); J. Stuart and N. Revett, *Antiquities of Athens* II (London, 1787 (1789)); E. D. Clarke, *Travels in Various Countries of Europe, Asia and Africa* (2nd edn., London, 1810–23); J. C. Hobhouse, *A Journey through Albania and Other Provinces of Turkey in Europe and Asia to Constantinople* (London, 1813). These are discussed in D. Constantine, *Early Greek Travellers and the Hellenic Ideal* (Cambridge, 1984); F.-M. Tsigakou, *The Rediscovery of Greece: travellers and painters of the romantic era* (New York, 1981); H. Angelomatis-Tsougarakis, *The Eve of the Greek revival: British travellers' perceptions of early nineteenth-century Greece* (London, 1990).

The actions of Elgin and his agents on the Acropolis are analysed in detail by St Clair, *Lord Elgin and the Marbles*, and D. Williams in ' "Of Publick utility and publick property": Lord Elgin and the Parthenon Sculptures', in A. Tsingarida (ed.), *Appropriating Antiquity* (Brussels, 2002); there is a briefer account in Cook, *The Elgin Marbles*. A franker than usual account of the War of Independence is offered by D. Brewer, *The Flame of Freedom: the Greek War of Independence 1821–1833* (London, 2001). R. Carter explains Schinkel's proposals for Otto's palace in 'Karl Friedrich Schinkel's project for a royal palace on the Acropolis', *Journal of the Society of Architectural Historians* 38 (1979). The triumph of archaeology and the Acropolis pageant of 1834 are discussed in E. Bastea, *The Creation of Modern Athens: planning the myth* (Cambridge, 1999); the archaeological clearance campaigns in R. A. McNeal, 'Archaeology and the destruction of the later Athenian Acropolis', in *Antiquity* 65 (1991). J. J. Coulton, *Greek Architects at Work: problems of structure and design* (London, 1977) offers a sane judgement on the so-called 'optical refinements' and other aspects of the Parthenon's architecture. The Neronian inscription is the subject of K. K. Carroll, *The Parthenon Inscription* (Durham, NC, 1982). N. Balanos described his own programme of restoration in *Les monuments de l'Acropole: relèvement et conservation* (Paris, 1938). The current restorations are discussed in R. Economakis (ed.), *Acropolis Restoration: the CCAM intervention* (London, 1994).

CHAPTER 5

The Sound and Light show is expertly decoded by E. Marlowe, 'Cold War illuminations of the classical past: "the Sound and Light Show" on the Athenian Acropolis', *Art History* 24 (2001). My own approach to Athenian democracy is not unlike R. Osborne's in 'Athenian democracy: something to celebrate?', in *Dialogos* 1 (1994); rather more celebratory is J. Dunn (ed.), *Democracy: the unfinished journey 508 BC – AD 1993* (New York, 1992). The inventories of the Parthenon are translated and discussed by D. Harris, *The Treasures of the Parthenon and Erechtheion* (Oxford, 1995).

The frieze has prompted an enormous amount of writing. An excellent introduction is I. Jenkins, *The Parthenon Frieze* (London, 1994); also a useful overview is J. Neils, *The Parthenon Frieze* (Cambridge, 2001). Different interpretations are offered by: J. B. Connelly, 'Parthenon and *Parthenoi*: a mythological interpretation of the Parthenon frieze', in the

American Journal of Archaeology 100 (1996) (human sacrifice); J. Boardman and D. Finn, *The Parthenon and its Sculptures* (Austin, Tex., 1985) (memorial to Marathon); R. Osborne, 'The viewing and obscuring of the Parthenon frieze', in the *Journal of Hellenic Studies* 107 (1987); A. Stewart, *Art, Desire and the Body in Ancient Greece* (Cambridge, 1997); D. Castriota, *Myth, Ethos and Actuality: official art in fifth-century BC Athens* (Madison, Wis., 1992). The Panathenaic festival at which the goddess was given a new *peplos* is explored in J. Neils (ed.), *Worshipping Athena: Panathenaia and Parthenon* (Madison, Wis., 1996). An authoritative guide to the pediments is O. Palagia, *The Pediments of the Parthenon* (2nd edn., Leiden, 1998). E. B. Harrison tries to pin down the career and style of Pheidias in a chapter in O. Palagia and J. J. Pollitt (eds), *Personal Styles in Greek Sculpture* (Cambridge, 1996).

The ancient idea of a god is discussed in Bruit Zaidmann and Schmitt Pantel, *Religion in the Ancient Greek City*. The role of statues in envisaging ancient deities is central to R. Gordon's article, 'The real and the imaginary: production and religion in the Graeco-Roman world', *Art History* 2 (1979) (reprinted in his *Image and Value in the Graeco-Roman World* (Aldershot, 1996)) and D. Tarn Steiner, *Images in Mind: statues in archaic and classical Greek literature and thought* (Princeton, 2001).

CHAPTER 6

The debates of 1816 (and the cleaning of the 1930s) are discussed in St Clair, *Lord Elgin and the Marbles*, with a robust response by J. Boardman, 'The Elgin Marbles: matters of fact and opinion' in the *International Journal of Cultural Property* 9 (2000); and in C. Hitchens, *The Elgin Marbles: should they be returned to Greece?* (2nd edn., London, 1998). The changing display of the Elgin Marbles in the British Museum is one of the major themes of I. Jenkins, *Archaeologists and Aesthetes in the Sculpture Galleries of the British Museum 1800–1939* (London, 1992). The surface of the marbles and the question of paint is discussed by I. Jenkins and A. D. Middleton, 'Paint on the Parthenon sculptures', *Annual of the British School at Athens* 83 (1988); this is developed in Jenkins's account of the 'Duveen cleaning', *Cleaning and Controversy: the Parthenon sculptures 1811–1939* (British Museum Occasional Papers 146, 2001). Other contributions to this debate include W. St Clair, 'The Elgin Marbles: questions of stewardship and accountability', in the *International Journal of Cultural Property* 8 (1999), and various lectures given at the 1999 conference now published on the British Museum's website (www.thebritishmuseum.ac.uk). Y. Hamilakis, 'Stories from exile: fragments from the cultural biography of the Parthenon (or "Elgin") marbles', in *World Archaeology* 31 (1999) stands above the fray to analyse the cultural significance of arguments about the Elgin Marbles.

LIST OF ILLUSTRATIONS

LIST OF FIGURES

GREEK NAMES

People have argued for centuries about how best to write Greek names in English. Some hard-line purists now insist on sticking as close to the original Greek letters as possible – so preferring 'Thoukudides' to the more familiar 'Thucydides', or 'Plutarchos' to 'Plutarch'. Most of the early travellers to the Parthenon discussed in this book had quite other ideas. In fact, a good number of them tried as hard as they could to by-pass Greek names and spelling entirely – calling the monument not the 'temple of Athena' but the 'temple of Minerva' (Athena's Roman equivalent). The picture gets even more complicated if we include Roman, French, German, Italian and Turkish writers. This book is about two and a half millennia of history with all its different spellings. As the sharp-eyed reader will discover, my own versions of Greek names are inevitably a compromise between consistency, accuracy and simple intelligibility.

ACKNOWLEDGEMENTS

This book has been fun to research and write. For that, thanks are due to Angelos Delivorrias, David Holton, Manolis Korres, Kostas Mavrakakis and Maria Vassilaki in Greece; in (or from) England, to Bryer, Nigel Cassidy, Robin Cormack, Tony Cutler, Peter Green, John Henderson, Ian Jenkins, Alan LeQuire, Dimitris Livanios, Robin Osborne, Anthony Snodgrass, Chris Stray and all the others who shared their Parthenon experiences. Both the British Museum and the Benaki have been generous with their resources and expertise. Finally, my friends at Profile Books – Peter Carson, Penny Daniel and Andrew Franklin, with Peter Campbell, Kate Griffin and Trevor Horwood – have sent this book into the world with characteristic skill and good humour.

INDEX